PRAISE FOR
TACTICAL SEO

'Having up-to-date information with a focus on key holistic and future-proof approaches is key to your success. The process-driven and value-based approach to SEO in this book is right on the money and will be valid for years to come.'
Steve Lock, Global Head of SEO, Sage Group

'A clear and easy-to-read knowledge base for anyone who wants to unlock the secrets of the SEO world. With practical tips and all the jargon clearly explained, this is great content for experts and novices alike.'
Kris Bezzant, Senior Vice President, HR, Capgemini

'Tactical SEO is a one-stop shop for everything a business should need to know about bringing their site to the top of the search rankings and helping it stay there.'
Richard Towey, Head of Content, PerformanceIN

'Lee Wilson explains exactly how to do SEO right: from getting started to measuring its success to taking result-driven action. This book will always be first off the shelf whenever you're working on an SEO project.'
Aki Libo-on, Assistant Editor, *Search Engine Journal*

'Lee is a meticulous, thought-inspiring, digital marketing professional and *Tactical SEO* is a true reflection of just that. Showcasing an enviable depth of SEO knowledge throughout, Lee explains not just how to understand search engines, but provides practical takeaways and priceless information to help you successfully manage and communicate the importance of SEO in our modern digital world. This publication is a great journey through the frequent changes that continue to occur in search marketing and how to positively act on them. I'd recommend this book for those taking their first steps into SEO, all the way through to those looking to take a completely refreshed approach to organic search as a channel. A reminder that now more than ever, we still have to think outside the box to stand out in search engines.'
Jack Cooper, Digital Marketing Manager, Strawberry Soup

'*Tactical SEO* not only provides an up-to-date overview of SEO marketplace, it brings together worldwide range of methods and tactics that can be used as a blueprint for training new and veteran SEOs ensuring that they are working in effective and efficient ways.'
Sam Osborne, Technical SEO specialist and blogger,
Vertical Leap / equilater.al

'SEO has evolved and is continually evolving. What was once best practice can now be deemed as spamming and Google will remove your search rankings. Tactical SEO gives you an up to the moment analysis of tactics to enable you to reach readers and customers through organic or paid search.'
Tim Hughes, CEO and Founder of The Social Selling Network and co-author
of *Social Selling*

'Lee's *Tactical SEO* is a truly actionable war chest for any modern day SEO consultant; his ability to simplify and digest even the most complex aspects of SEO makes this book not only a handbook for everyday use, but also a great testimony to the fact that SEO isn't dead and is better than ever.'
Krystian Szastok, SEO Freelancer and Agency Owner, Arise Digitally,
krystianszastok.co.uk

'*Tactical SEO* offers an unrivalled journey through the basics of catering for Google and onto advanced considerations like setting your website up for the long term and contingency planning. For a combination of ground-level learning and wisdom that only an experienced SEO expert can impart, it's a hugely important read.'
Richard Towey, Head of Content, PerformanceIN

Tactical SEO

Dedication

*Each word in this book was written because of
my daughter Sophia and my wife Ayako,
who inspire me to have passions in life –
and to act upon them. Every day they motivate me
to try to become a better human being.*

*And to my mum and dad who have always given
both myself and my brother, Kye, everything
they never had themselves, and so much more.*

Tactical SEO
The theory and practice of search marketing

Lee Wilson

KoganPage

LONDON PHILADELPHIA NEW DELHI

First published in Great Britain and the United States in 2016 by Kogan Page Limited

2nd Floor, 45 Gee Street	1518 Walnut Street, Suite 1100	4737/23 Ansari Road
London	Philadelphia PA 19102	Daryaganj
EC1V 3RS	USA	New Delhi 110002
United Kingdom		India

© Lee Wilson 2016

ISBN   978 0 7494 7799 8
E-ISBN 978 0 7494 7800 1

British Library Cataloguing-in-Publication Data

A CIP record for this book is available from the British Library.

Library of Congress Control Number

2016946121

Typeset by Graphicraft Limited, Hong Kong
Print production managed by Jellyfish
Printed and bound in Great Britain by CPI Group (UK) Ltd, Croydon CR0 4YY

CONTENTS

LIST OF FIGURES AND TABLES

ABOUT THE AUTHOR

Lee has been actively involved with online marketing since the early 2000s, and has headed up online and digital departments for over a decade. Currently, Head of SEO for one of the United Kingdom's most established digital agencies (Vertical Leap), Lee has worked on the agency side of SEO delivery since 2010.

Prior to delivering digital marketing within an agency environment, Lee worked in house for a number of years, as well as spending time setting up and running a limited company providing website and digital marketing solutions.

Lee has been managing teams since the age of 16, and takes a great deal of personal and professional pride in the progression of others he has managed through learning, training and development.

Lee loves writing about the digital industry, especially SEO, in which he has specialized for a number of years. He engages on the topic with people daily – and he frequently writes content on expert industry websites.

Although not a fan of heights, Lee also likes to challenge himself, becoming regularly involved with various fundraising and voluntary events as well as personal challenges such as bungie jumping and abseiling, to help causes he believes in.

Most important though, are the many happy hours spent chasing after his young daughter Sophia, born in 2013 and the light in his life.

Lee can be contacted at **twitter.com/LWilson1980** and **www.linkedin.com/in/leewilson1980**

ACKNOWLEDGEMENTS

My passion for digital marketing has led, inevitably, to the writing of this book. There are gaps in the way in which the SEO industry is projected and understood, and very little coverage on the *why* behind the *what*, when it comes to the delivery of organic results online. Long before the creation of this book, many people have been influential in making it happen.

Since the early 2000s I have had the privilege of working with some truly brilliant people. Every single one of them has added to the realization of this book; however, I know for a fact that very few of them will want or claim any recognition for the role they have played.

For the support offered throughout, and the learning curve that led me to this point, I must thank Vertical Leap – my place of employment for a number of years. Special mentions include Matt Hopkins and the board of directors, everyone in the SEO team (of course), plus the people in the company who, each and every day, add to the unique culture that empowers people constantly to question the status quo, and to grow both personally and professionally.

I've been lucky to have some very close friends who have always been present. I know that by mentioning some of them individually, I will be omitting many others, but I have to say a special thanks to Russ Garland, Jon Caton and Ben Curtis.

Finally, any opportunity to acknowledge the important people in my life, whether professionally or personally, will always come back to the people that make *everything* what it is: Ayako, Sophia, mum, dad and Kye.

Re-evaluating SEO

LEARNING OUTCOMES

After reading this chapter you will have greater understanding and confidence in:

- What SEO is

- Why SEO matters

- SEO servicing basic business needs

- The human attributes of SEO

- The value of earning results

Most people who are aware of the term Search Engine Optimization (SEO) have some understanding, or a preconceived notion, of what SEO is, why it matters, and probably also a basic understanding of the difference between paid and earned (or free) results.

Having worked in the industry from the early 2000s, I have witnessed an ever growing number of business and marketing professionals, students, directors, company owners and digital enthusiasts, all taking their initial steps into delivery of SEO (outsourced or in-house). They almost always have one thing in common when it comes to SEO, and that is snippets of SEO knowledge driving strategy.

Figure 1.1 reflects the extremes of this snippet knowledge in practise. At one end of this timeline we have *outdated* (or dated) *SEO*. The focus of this being, single keyword prioritization, volume-based link building, plus highly targeted ranking goals. After discussing what SEO is, this chapter also defines 'dated SEO' in more detail.

At the other end of the timeline we have *on-trend SEO*. The focus of this being, the latest Google update or mainstream industry blog post, combined with a constant readjustment of approach.

FIGURE 1.1   Snippet knowledge SEO – timeline extremes

The aspect that is missing, and what these 'snippet knowledge' based approaches omit entirely (regardless of where they fall on the timeline) is the *why* behind the *what*. For example, a deeper logical understanding of the context and purpose of the actions completed, as opposed to the completion of actions in isolation.

It is the application of the *why* context that forms the constant throughout the process of creating effective SEO strategy, and forms a continual thread throughout this book.

What is SEO?

The starting point of any investment in SEO – whether this *investment* is in the shape of capital investment or time and resource investment – should be to answer the primary question: What is SEO? If you ask 10 digital experts this question, the likelihood is that you will get several variations on a main theme.

What is Search Engine Optimization (SEO)?

Search Engine Optimization (SEO) is the application of specialist expertise for the purpose of increasing the quality and quantity of organic (earned, natural or free) traffic from search engines to a web page or website.

When you take steps to segment the question 'what is SEO?' into its component parts, SEO starts to become much more meaningful.

Application

It is the application of specialist insight which can be the barrier or the catalyst for much of the success or failure of an SEO strategy. If there is a lack of focus on the type of actions completed, the results will often be disjointed at best, and at worst impossible to attribute (or repeat) for the next phases of potential gains. Excessive strategy without action will repeatedly lead to missed opportunities.

Expertise

As a form of marketing, SEO is certainly in its infancy compared to more established and traditional areas of expertise. Having said this, the speed at which the SEO industry changes and the low barriers to market entry, have resulted in one of the most competitive and potentially rewarding marketplaces for advertising, accessible on a global scale.

Visibility

Although not detailed explicitly in the above definition, organic search traffic cannot be achieved without visibility. In this context, visibility refers to impressions. Put simply, this is the number of times your organic adverts appear in the search engine results pages (SERPs). Assuming relevancy is present in new areas of visibility, it is the extra impressions that will directly lead to traffic gains and ultimately end results achieved.

Quality

The fact that the above definition placed quality before quantity was very deliberate. Traffic volumes are only effective if the quality of the traffic supports some likelihood of a direct end result. Quality can be measured in a number of ways including click-through rate (CTR), time on site, average page views, micro or macro conversions and more.

Quantity

Once the quality criteria have been satisfied, increasing the amount of quality traffic to the web page or website is one of the key performance metrics for every SEO project. It is almost impossible to manage an effective SEO campaign over a long period without gaining extra volumes of traffic.

Organic (traffic)

Often referred to as free, natural or earned traffic, the term 'organic' relates to the section of the SERPs that does not incur any cost per click (ie it is unpaid traffic). Undoubtedly, it is the cumulative value of driving greater volumes of relevant and free traffic which places SEO at the heart of many companies' marketing mix.

The percentage share of the available total click opportunity between organic, paid and other click actions will always vary; however, common correlations between data sources reviewed, place organic click share between 45 per cent and 50 per cent of the total SERP opportunity.

FIGURE 1.2   The click share of a typical search engine results page

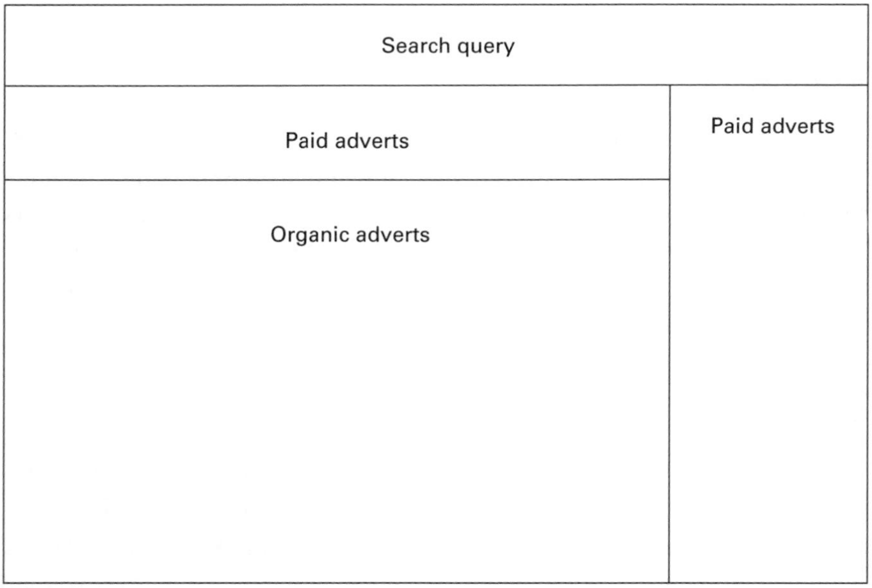

Search query	
Paid adverts	Paid adverts
Organic adverts	

Search engines

Google, Bing and Yahoo! are all examples of search engines.

A search engine is a class, or group of programs that seek out and explore items (usually content types) which exist in the specific search index (or database) and have a correlation to a user query raised. In most cases the returned result to a user query takes the form of a web page or website on the world wide web (www). At this point it is worth noting that 'internet' as a www. is a protocol which is not required for a website to exist.

It is important to note that a search engine returns results to search queries driven by the information *currently* contained within that engine's search index. A search engine index will never contain all of the information available, and will never be 100 per cent up to date. The volume and speed at which new content is discovered, indexed and potentially displayed is rapidly increasing, but it will never be a completely live information feed.

Web page (website)

A web page is an individual (in most cases a hypertext) file available to view using browsers on the world wide web. Web pages often contain a varied mix of content types and associated files for scripts and graphics, and hyperlink to and from other web pages or documents on the web.

A website is a collection of web pages, usually structured in a hierarchical or logical way, and related to a specific entity (be that a person, a business or any other identifiable bonding relation) usually focused on a single or dominant topic.

What is dated SEO?

Dated SEO can cover many areas and a few of the more common dated tactics are discussed in more detail below. These dated approaches to SEO delivery should be avoided.

The SEO industry changes quickly and failure to keep up to date with the industry as it develops can lead to negative algorithm impact, manual Google penalties, and limited search success.

One thing to note is that there is a difference between 'dated SEO' and 'black hat SEO' – and a large part of this comes down to intent.

Black hat SEO in its basic form relates to the use of strategies that clearly violate the guidelines of the main search engines (most notably Google). In most instances black hat SEO is associated with very short-term tactics with very little, if any, real acknowledgement or focus on the actual users you are (or should be) optimizing. Black hat SEO is almost fully focused on search engines only, with limited user value gained as a direct outcome of the actions completed.

Dated SEO encompasses many of the same tactics deployed for search engine wins as seen in black hat SEO. However, often the intent behind the tactics is not to cheat (or game) the search engines for artificial success, but to deliver search engine optimization from a limited level of shallow information or limited depth of current knowledge or expertise. The adage 'a little knowledge can be a dangerous thing' is very true when looking at servicing SEO needs for businesses.

Single keyword focus

There is a significant difference between optimizing for keywords within content and topic focus areas, and having an excessive focus on exact match single term (or very targeted and limited term) delivery in SEO. When creating content for your website, it is important to complete keyword research to really understand user needs and to pitch the content accordingly. Optimizing content requires knowledge of keyword usage and maximization. Repeatedly using the same keywords in content for the purposes of ranking for that single term is a dated tactic that has limited long-term potential. When you are creating content, consider the following questions as this will help to identify whether you are too keyword-focused.

Are there other pages on the website with similar content?

When you have website landing pages created for the purpose of ranking for a refined set of keywords it becomes very challenging to differentiate the purpose and value of one page from the next.

Tip: Read your similar content pages, remove the repeated keyword (or small grouping of keywords) and objectively consider if the remaining content offers anything distinctly of value. If it does not, you are probably focusing excessively on exact match, or single keywords.

Is there much term variation on your website copy?

An indicator of depth of content is the natural phrase and term variations that are visible in the content. When you read a quality article, journal or research paper, you would not be able to see within second's optimization intent, and the same needs to be true for every piece of digital content you create.

Tip: Copy and paste your website content into a Word doc and find (in Word Ctrl + F) all the instances of the exact match keyword. Look at how frequently this term appears compared to the remainder of the other relevant terms (excluding adjoining terms). If there is a clear weighting, you will likely need to revisit the content, add in variations and synonyms and likely, another few levels of user-driven worth.

Would you speak to someone in the same way you have written your content?

It can be a valuable exercise to read your content out loud. If you work in an open-plan office environment this may be slightly more challenging, but your content quality will increase when you add this simple step into your editorial process.

It becomes almost embarrassing to read aloud excessively keyword-focused content because it is so apparent that either the content created has very minimal standalone value, or that the content has not been created with people in mind.

Tip: When you write content, leave at least a few hours between the first draft content creation and its actual live publication. During this time, take on other non-related tasks. Come back to the content and read it out loud. Book a meeting room if you are conscious of people seeing you talking to yourself, and imagine you are speaking this same content to another person (ideally someone whose opinion you value highly). If you feel even slightly embarrassed by what you are writing, do not publish that content – consider keyword usage and rework it with the user in mind.

Are you using keyword density tools?

A keyword density tool is a means to provide a percentage (stat) to measure the number of times a specific keyword is mentioned on a web page compared to the total number of other terms on that same page. This may include references in code as well as text, or in body content in isolation.

First, there are valid reasons for using keyword density tools for improving SEO performance and identifying excessive key term focus. This question should be considered, to assess why you are using a keyword density tool.

If you have target percentages for keyword inclusion in content, or believe that you have an optimal keyword density, you are potentially walking a very thin line between optimizing and spamming.

Hiding content

When you add something to your website, that content – whatever its form – will usually have an intended audience. If you are adding content to your website and masking it, or hiding it from users, you need to consider what you are doing and why you are doing it. By hiding content (eg content that has been styled in the same colour as the background of the page making it invisible to user), the website is servicing one aspect of search engine optimization with complete avoidance of the user (something to be avoided).

Another example may be styling links so that they appear as standard content even though they have link functionality.

There are legitimate reasons to hide some content. As an example you may have repeated content (eg financial services terms and conditions that may need to be read by the user on all services and product pages) that you do not want to detract from the particular purpose of the page. This type of content may be hidden from view, and may require extra user action to view it (eg clicking on 'read more', a tab of content, or other functionality). As with many of these dated tactics, there can be valid reasons for using them. The purpose of being aware of the negative uses is for self-evaluation. You should question whether the tactic you are using is the right one, or whether it is likely to be potentially damaging to search engine success over the longer term.

If you are hiding content from the user the main questions to ask yourself are:

- Why don't I want the user want to see this content?
- What is the need for the content?/Who is this content for?
- What am I hoping to achieve with this content?

Doorway pages

Also known as bridge pages, gateway pages, and by a few other names, a doorway page is a web page created to spam the search engine results pages with low quality and very low user value content in order to rank highly and pass that traffic onto another web page or location. These can often be seen in location pages with zero unique value that repeat the same small set of keywords excessively and redirect to another destination after the user clicks on the search engine advert. There can be good reason to use these pages, but you if you do make use of them you should ask yourself:

- What is the purpose of the doorway pages?
- Are the pages for people or for search engines?
- Is the focus and value of the page very restricted, or is the intention to drive lots of generic traffic to the page?
- Do the pages have standalone value or are they simply watered down versions of other deeper content pages on the site?
- Can people visiting these pages access the remainder of the website's main content, or are they limiting the user experience?

Duplicate content

Also referred to as scraped or copied content, duplicate content is any content that is originated on other websites that you include in part (large parts of content rather than small snippets or references) or in full on your website with or without express permission, or in many cases not referring to the content creator source. The intended outcome from this duplication is to drive search engine rankings and likely impressions, traffic and sales from that content without investment in its creation. Duplicate content can also refer to content that exists on other sections and pages within your own website.

When it comes to duplicate content consider the following questions:

- What is causing the duplication? It could be other sites scraping your content, it could be your content management system (CMS) creating multiple versions of pages, and it could be you intentionally copying other website content for leveraging artificial search gains – there are many other scenarios that can fall into this area of self-review.

- Do you have a number of pages on your site with limited user or content value outside of the website template?

- Is all of your website content accessible for crawling and indexation?

- Do you promote your content in its entirety, or large parts of it on external websites?

Low-quality link building

This includes creating masses of high-volume and low-quality links, link farms and irrelevant link building. It also involves repeatedly seeking external links from other websites for the purpose of passing authority to your site (and ultimately fake or artificial search engine and ranking gains), regardless of the quality, relevancy, or audience perceived value. Links are one of the most important ranking signals for the major search engines to attribute value and relevancy to a web page or website, and while there are many effective and required link-building tactics necessary to support SEO objectives, quality is a defining measurement. When you consider low-quality link building, some of the key questions to ask yourself are:

- What is the goal of the link?
- Is the link activity against Google guidelines?
- Would you be happy justifying the link in a face-to-face meeting?

- Will the link drive referral traffic to your website?
- How relevant is the linking website?
- How frequently is this website linking to you?
- What anchor text is being used and why?
- How many different types of backlinks does your website have?
- Where do most external linking point to on your website?
- How much trust and authority do the external linking domains have?
- Are all links passing authority?

Paid links

You can buy links or almost any form of advertorial content on external websites and drive referral traffic to your website. That is a valid form of paid marketing and there is nothing wrong with this technique as part of your multi-channel marketing strategy. Where there is an issue, however, is in any failure to handle paid links appropriately. Paid links should be clearly labelled as such and should not pass authority (or PageRank). The passing of value through buying and selling of links is in direct violation of the Google guidelines and can lead to website penalization, including substantial rankings loss from algorithmic and manual Google penalties. All paid links need to have the rel='nofollow' attribute adding to hyperlinks. If you are giving or receiving value (not just monetary value, although this is the most common form of link payment), you should ask yourself:

- Is there any payment form involved in link creation?
- Are all paid links clearly labelled as such?
- Do any paid links pass authority or PageRank?
- Are you using the rel='nofollow' attribute correctly?

Why does SEO matter?

SEO provides visibility. It brings people to your storefront and encourages them to come in. SEO constantly maintains your premises, looks to improve your communication skills with your customers and gives your messaging meaning.

Through SEO you can discover what your customers want and when. You can find new opportunities for market share and satisfy them.

SEO enables you to compete against the biggest budgets, the global brands and the fiercest business models.

On top of all of this, SEO is free and it never requires rest, relaxation, days off or six or more hours' sleep every evening.

In light of the above, the reason why SEO matters is that your business needs it. It is these basic business *needs* for SEO which are explored in more detail next.

SEO services business critical needs

Every company, whether revenue driven or 'not for profit', has a number of basic needs that enable it to function – regardless of industry. SEO, when applied correctly, completes an active supporting role, spanning a number of these business critical needs.

FIGURE 1.3 Model of basic business needs for SEO

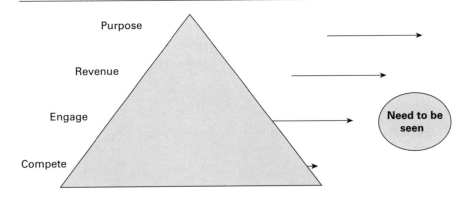

The need to be seen

Perhaps the most basic of company and website needs – certainly in the online environment – is visibility. Without question, this is the foundation for building upon all search success. If you are not appearing in relevant search niches online, you will not be able to drive traffic to your website.

The need to compete

If appearing more frequently online is the first barrier and the first need to fulfil, then competing online is the next. If you have a financial limit, regardless of how vast it may be, there will be a point at which you hit a paid ceiling. When this occurs you will need SEO for ranking effectively among your competition in a scalable way.

The need to engage

Seeing people peer into your shop window tells you there is a demand for what you do. Having footfall reinforces your ability to cater for that demand. The moment you move from appearing (pre-click visibility) through to engaging (post click), the challenge becomes one of matching expectations and providing a mutually effective solution that is user and business viable.

The need to generate revenue

Return on Investment (ROI) is the ultimate goal from almost every marketing activity and SEO is no different: turning impressions into visits and visits into sales. The efficiency and effectiveness of this process is the art of SEO.

The need to fulfil a purpose

None of the previous needs can be addressed, in part or in full, without a business purpose. Purpose helps to define strategy and is regularly a motivating force for any value proposition differentiator that supports success.

Once you go beyond the basic business needs for SEO, it becomes necessary to start to consider a few of the specialist roles that SEO provides. All of the following are human attributes for organization role fulfilment – this is an interesting point to note (ie the human attributes that SEO can deliver), before reading on.

FIGURE 1.4   The requirement for search engine optimization

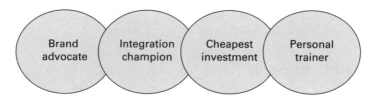

Your biggest brand advocate

SEO results are earned, rather than paid for. To the savvy searcher, this can place increased trust in the perceived value of the brands that are prolific in organic listings. Part of this trust attribution can be the awareness and acknowledgement of the predominantly value-based work required to appear repeatedly for relevant and competitive search phrases.

Every time you display for a search result, that information is tied to the URL displayed – tied to your brand. The more frequently you appear in conversation (in this context 'conversation' being between user and search engine, user and social network, or user and any other digital form of communication where SEO can impact visibility performance), the more SEO is directly and indirectly advocating your brand to the user.

When looking at metrics to support this statement, the most pertinent one is the often-correlated growth trend of direct traffic, which mirrors many successful SEO campaigns. To distil this further, you could also segment direct traffic into brand and non-brand. The expectation would be that brand direct traffic would exceed the growth of non-brand, because of this partnership of SEO and brand advocate.

To clarify, brand traffic is traffic that specifically mentions your brand name or a variation of the brand name. So, for example if my company name was 'Wilson Websites' brand traffic would be segmented into traffic including terms like: wilson websites, wilson, wilson sites etc.

Non-brand traffic therefore is everything excluding the brand name and variations of the brand.

A practical example of a business looking to increase brand awareness would be where Company A is a start-up organization; it has a great product, but it is a new concept, with limited external awareness. To generate initial buzz, the company incorporates a mixture of personal brand building (key staff within the company leveraging its expertise and existing personal networks and identity) and business brand building (primarily based on social media engagement and brand awareness tied to location and any current client base).

This combination of brand building tactics starts to lead to search impressions and traffic coming to the website (as well as other traffic types including referral traffic from social media and direct traffic from people typing in the website address directly into a search engine). All of this traffic is tied to the brand (business brand and personal brands associated with the business).

Your champion for integration

Every interaction with your website improves with SEO. When designing a new website, SEO brings a balance between style and substance. When combined with user experience, SEO provides insight from data that is needed in the form that best serves the user.

For content creators, SEO encourages logic-powered writing and a means to leverage the value from each written word. SEO bonds expertise through the common goal of making things better.

The reason why it is more logical to allocate the integration value more to SEO than any of the previous roles identified, is that you can very specifically identify and isolate each of the others' involvement, but SEO flows as a constant through them all.

Your cheapest investment

When you invest capital in SEO, the *free* nature of impressions and clicks means that accumulated success can deliver the cheapest returns on investment. Unlike paid advertising, the only expense incurred with visibility gained is fulfilling that demand effectively. That said, traffic received from SEO does come at another price. It generally brings with it higher user expectations.

Users demand accessibility and speed of delivery, regardless of the device used. People must have relevancy of results and clear immediate value far exceeding a shallow response, to match their search query.

The often enticing opportunity to bounce (or pogo stick) from one website back to the SERPs and onto another website, means that the window of opportunity to capture visitor ROI is small – but one that you can enlarge with the right approach.

Your website's personal trainer

Regardless of age, size or location, every website needs a regular health check and a repeat prescription. Technical SEO builds your website's core strength, improving resistance to website hacking and site downtime. Through constant improvement, and by sustaining of your site's technical performance, you encourage results that transcend search verticals, geo locations and reputation.

There are many analogies that can be used to compare SEO to another entity – one is that of a human being.

Humans need regular health checks to make sure that nothing is overlooked for too long without remedy (ie traditional technical SEO for websites). If you neglect the health of a particular part of the human body, it will start to function less effectively (for websites this could include site speed and broken links – but you may apply this more broadly to underperforming pages as well).

When you add mass to the skeletal framework you have to consider the impact of this on performance (mass could easily be seen as new pages being added, or something changing like inclusion of video content on a website).

Then, consider things such as fresh quality content being the fuel for a website, equivalent to types of food consumed that fuels the human body. And the first impression time frame that people and websites have to capture the desired attention of the people they engage with.

Understanding the value of earning results

This section focuses on a deeper understanding of why earning success online through organic search engine optimization (SEO) matters. It is *not* about comparing paid, owned and earned media types.

> ## Why does earning results online really matter?
>
> When you earn something it matters. It takes expertise, resource, innovation and effort to earn organic results. There is no way to sustain longevity of SEO success without these component parts. When you earn something, you gain a sense of achievement that reflects the effort used to deserve the results delivered. When you earn something online, you often gather direct and indirect business benefits from it too.

Earned results encourage customer-generated content (CGC)

Also widely referred to as 'UGC' (user-generated content), one of the most visible signals of earned search success is the content created, shared and engaged with *not* developed by you (your business or your website). Types of customer-generated content are varied, but the main content areas relevant to earned results include reviews, testimonials, social PR, forums and user- (or consumer-) generated case studies.

The value gained from CGC will differ. However, it tends to have the largest direct impact at the bottom of the funnel, where people are looking to gather the final trust signals required in order to make a new purchase decision. When a business is able to be associated with external votes of confidence in the form of CGC, the value or earning results becomes directly measurable in terms of ROI.

Earning positive PR by adding value to your audience

When you complete something of value and make that value visible to the audiences which matters most (to your business and probably its bottom line), it is not uncommon to capture, measure and gather results from positive PR.

Earned PR is usually initiated from the development of something tangible (often personal created content, or the free delivery of expert opinion and advice) for the purposes of reach and engagement.

Hard work keeps your website healthy

One of the most frequently used strategies for earning long-term success online is through in-depth content creation. White papers, guides, detailed reporting and other labour-intensive content types, all add user significance that would not be as viable in any other results niche outside of earned marketing channels.

This comes back to the fact that every new click reduces your cost per click. While organic traffic is never 100 per cent free (as some form of outlay will always be required), freeing up capital to invest in generating larger volumes of new earned results will always be more feasible in an organic medium, in contrast to any other cost-based model.

It is this *value-to-earned results cycle* which sits at the centre of the metrics delivered from earning online success.

FIGURE 1.5 Value to earned results cycle in organic metric success

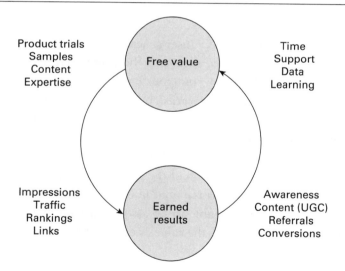

Key terms

The following key terms have been explained in more detail to support a thorough understanding of the items discussed earlier in this chapter. For ease of reference, all of the definitions are listed in the order that they first appear in this chapter.

Search engine optimization (SEO)

Search Engine Optimization (SEO) is the application of specialist expertise for the purpose of increasing the quality and quantity of organic (earned, natural or free) traffic from search engines to a web page or website.

Black hat SEO

Black hat SEO in its basic form relates to the use of strategies that clearly violate the main search engines (and mostly notably Google) guidelines. In most instances black hat SEO is associated with very short-term tactics with very little, if any, real acknowledgement or focus on the actual users you are (or should be) optimising for. Black hat SEO is almost fully focused towards search engines only, with limited user value gained as a direct outcome of the actions completed.

Dated SEO

Dated SEO encompasses many of the same tactics deployed for search engine wins as seen in black hat SEO. Frequently, however, the intent behind the tactics is not to cheat (or game) the search engines for artificial success, but to deliver search engine optimization from a limited level of shallow information or a limited depth of knowledge.

Keyword density tools

A keyword density tool is a way to give you a percentage (stat) to measure the number of times a specific keyword is mentioned on a web page compared to the total number of other terms on that same page. Tools will differ in many ways both in features and processes used to determine keyword density. For example, whether they include adjoining terms or not, as well as other factors such as incorporating term use in code or just body content, and more.

Doorway pages

Also known as bridge pages, gateway pages, and by a few other names, a doorway page is a web page created to spam the search engine results pages with low quality and very low user value content in order to rank highly and pass that traffic onto another web page or location. These can often be seen in location pages with zero unique value that repeat the same small set of keywords excessively and redirect to another destination after the user clicks on the search engine advert.

Duplicate content

Also referred to as scraped or copied content, duplicate content is any content that is originated on other websites that you include on your website in part (large parts of content rather than small snippets or references) or in full, with or without express permission, or in many cases, not referring to the content creator source. Duplicate content can also refer to content that exists on other sections and pages within your own website.

Low-quality link building

This includes creating masses of high-volume and low-quality links, link farms and irrelevant link building. This also involves repeatedly seeking external links from other websites for the purpose of passing authority to your site (and ultimately fake or artificial search engine and ranking gains), regardless of the quality, relevancy, or audience perceived value.

Outsource

Making a decision to use the services of an external supplier. This may be in the form of some of the component parts of the service, or the service as a whole.

In-house

Deciding to build into an existing team or company the expertise or ability required.

Strategy

A set of actions forming a plan which has a desired outcome or end goal – strategies can be short, medium or longer term.

Investment

Relating to the use of cash (or other form of payment) for an expected increase on initial outlay. Typically, this refers to getting an increase in money used for a service provided.

Return on investment (ROI)

This is the benefit obtained from the person/business/entity who risked the initial investment for the services provided. The greater the ROI, the more profitable the investment.

Advocate (brand)

A person, business or other entity that publicly provides positive sentiment towards a product, person or service.

Direct traffic

The traffic that comes to your web page or website without any previous referring source. This is typically from people directly typing your website address (URL) into a browser address bar, or from the use of bookmarked content.

Integration

Working together (in collaboration), for a joint goal, purpose or end result. It is often said that the value of integrated working far exceeds the gains delivered from isolated working approaches to delivery.

Key points

- Search Engine Optimization (SEO) is the application of specialist expertise for the purpose of increasing the quality and quantity of organic (earned, natural or free) traffic from search engines to a web page or website.

- It is the application of the *why* context that forms the constant throughout the process of creating effective SEO strategy.

- Every company, regardless of industry, and whether revenue driven or 'not for profit', has a number of basic needs that will enable it to function: the need to be seen; the need to compete; the need to engage; the need to generate revenue and the need to fulfil a purpose.

- It takes expertise, resource, innovation and effort to earn organic results. There is no way to sustain long-term SEO success without these component parts.

- One of the most prolific strategies used for earning long-term success online is through in-depth content creation.

Understanding Google

02

LEARNING OUTCOMES

By the time you have completed this chapter you will have a greater understanding of the practical value of:

- The fundamentals of the Google ethos
- The symbiotic nature of Google and SEO
- Applying a checklist approach to optimizing for Google
- Why other search engines matter

How much do you really know about Google?

Before delving into the fundamentals of the Google ethos, it is useful to have a good overview of the company.

Founded in 1998, Google had revenue in excess of $55 billion by 2014. By 2015, Google had been sitting in the number one position of the Fortune. com '100 Best Companies to Work For' for six years, having been included in this prestigious list for nine years. In the United States alone, Google employs over 40,000 staff, with many more across the globe.

The name of the search engine was originally based on the word *googol*, a mathematical representation of a 1 followed by 100 zeros.

Although Google is well known for its paid revenue model, its first paid adverts appeared in 2000, growing from text-only adverts to include mobile, video and many other sponsored advertising alternatives.

The Googleplex (Google physical headquarters) is based in Mountain View, California; but, of course, Google also has a global physical presence. Despite its global dominance, Google still strives to maintain the type of culture seen traditionally with many successful start-ups – one of creativity, freedom and innovation, supported by a fun environment empowering staff to take on calculated risks and challenge the status quo. Interwoven throughout the Google culture is the encouragement of people diversity, equality and inclusion.

Why is it important to understand Google?

Google dominates global search. Google's market share is more than three times that of its nearest competitor in the United States and arguably it is even more dominant in the United Kingdom.[1]

The fundamentals of the Google ethos

The Google manifesto, entitled the 'Ten things we know to be true', is the basis for any interpretation of the Google ethos. This manifesto is understood to have been created not long after the company was formed, and has reportedly held true ever since. The following 10 points underpin the Google philosophy and are directly relevant to search engine success.[2]

Everything stems from user focus

Despite Google being a hugely successful revenue-generating entity, the guiding principle of the company is that revenue comes as a result of servicing the user, not as a competing force, and not to the detriment of the user.

The meaning of the above statement is apparent when you look at the Google approach to delivering search engine results.

There is a clear distinction between paid and earned (or organic listings). This provides a direct means for the user to drive their search experience. The end user can decide to base a search journey from companies who have bid for position, and therefore are likely to be among the higher turnover organizations. Alternatively, the end user can drive their search journey using organic listings – those that have had to create authority, relevancy and likely, value specific to the user search query, for higher placement. The third choice for the user is a combination of both paid and organic results. This approach enables the user to consider the accumulated advantages of companies appearing in both prominent search areas.

With the exception of Google Doodles (these are the frequently changing Google logo items and sometimes interactive elements at the very top of the Google SERPs), you will notice how simple the search results pages are. Use of colour is limited and interactive distractions are very limited, meaning that the information provided is in a clear and repeated form.

When additional user value can be derived at search result delivery level (as opposed to post-click level), Google also includes new layers of information. Some examples of this include the Google Knowledge Graph, Carousel and Local Pack results.

The figures below provide examples of how these search display elements can be seen within the search results pages. At this stage, it becomes necessary to consider that these display changes will differ depending on the search query (more specifically the search query type), as well as the search engine geo targeting and many other variants.

This clear and simple delivery of results may not appear to be particularly significant; however, when you recall that the Google revenue model is one of paid advertising, it is amazing that sponsored (or paid) adverts do not employ user distraction to support increased revenue generation. Factors such as the absence of distractions are, of course, crucial to putting the end user first and Google gain second.

Figure 2.1 illustrates a basic search engine results page (SERP) incorporating the Google Knowledge Graph after you remove all of the data-complete

FIGURE 2.1   Alternative search engine results display options driven by the user – Google Knowledge Graph

Search query	
Organic adverts	Knowledge Graph
Organic adverts	Active white space

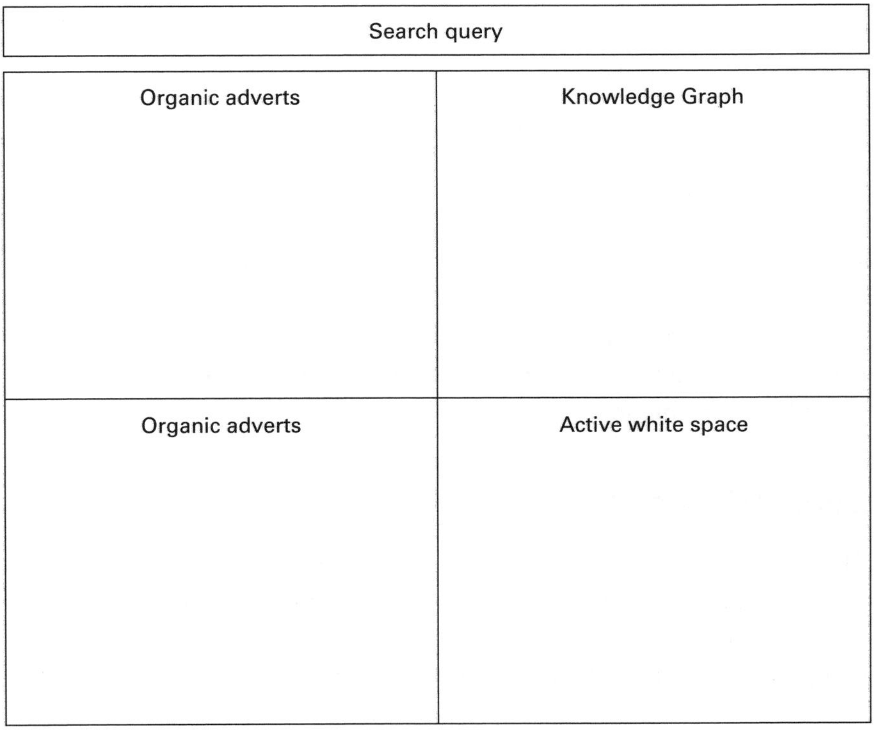

elements of the page and other component parts not tied to the positioning of this feature.

Figure 2.2 illustrates the Google search results, focusing on the inclusion element of Google Carousel.

FIGURE 2.2   Alternative search engine results display options driven by the user – Google Carousel

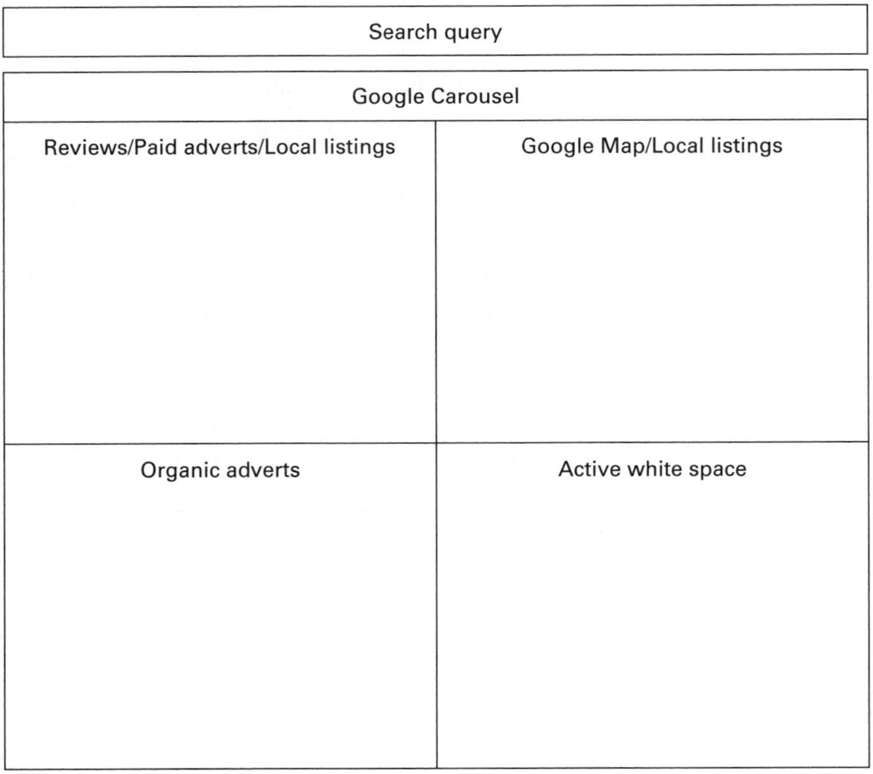

Search query	
Google Carousel	
Reviews/Paid adverts/Local listings	Google Map/Local listings
Organic adverts	Active white space

In Figure 2.3 you can see the main component parts of a Google search engine results page after you remove all visual elements and include Google Local Pack information.

Google do search

This is *the* focus of Google. Everything else Google delivers (whether a product such as Gmail, Maps or a supplemental service provided) is as a result of the constant attention to solving search needs. At the heart of this is the ethos of doing something better than anyone else.

FIGURE 2.3 Alternative search engine results display options driven by the user – Google Local Pack

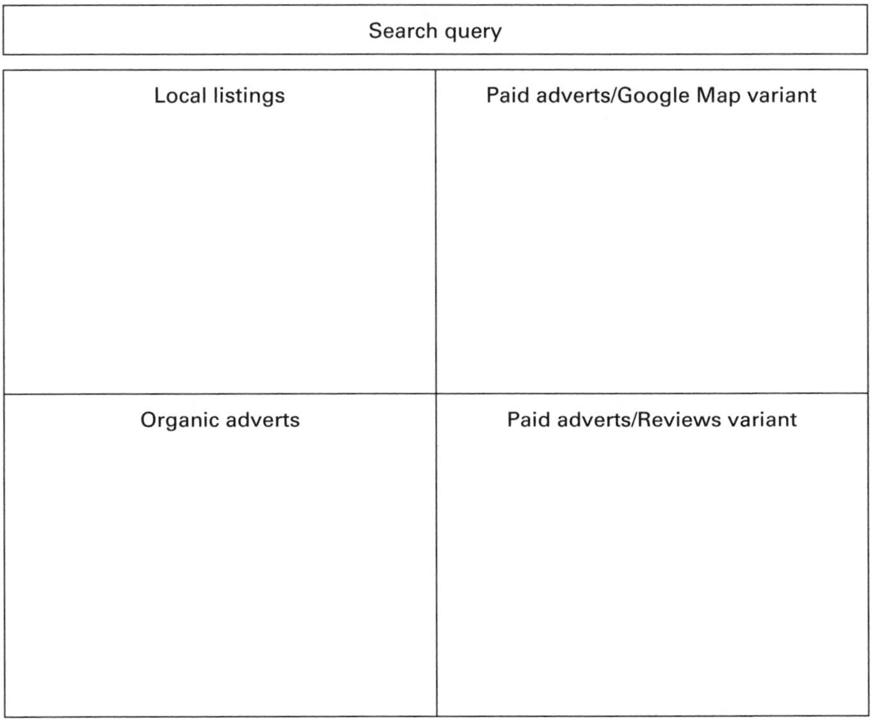

Search query	
Local listings	Paid adverts/Google Map variant
Organic adverts	Paid adverts/Reviews variant

At this stage it is important to see how other Google products all directly evolve from this continuous improvement approach to doing one thing extremely well (search), or come as an application of knowledge learnt from this mission.

Figure 2.4 shows a number of the Google products which have developed as a direct result of the focus on doing one thing extremely well – in this case search.

It is interesting to think about this statement – '*Google do search*'. Because of the great variety of other things that Google is now known for (Maps, Office, self-driving cars), it can be a challenge to identify the foundation on which all of this is built.

The focus on doing one thing extremely well has enabled Google to monopolize the search environment in almost every market where it has become a challenger to existing search competition. This is no more apparent than in English-speaking geo locations where Google often rolls out early phases of beta testing and more.

FIGURE 2.4 Single point product development model –
Google Search

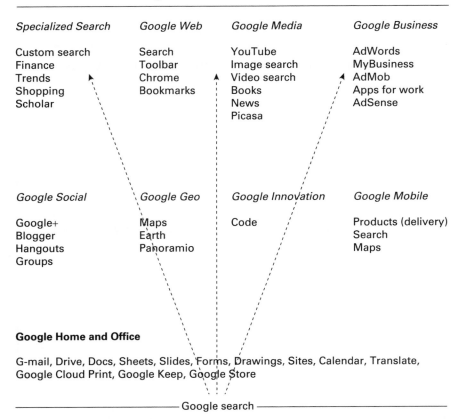

Specialized Search	Google Web	Google Media	Google Business
Custom search	Search	YouTube	AdWords
Finance	Toolbar	Image search	MyBusiness
Trends	Chrome	Video search	AdMob
Shopping	Bookmarks	Books	Apps for work
Scholar		News	AdSense
		Picasa	

Google Social	Google Geo	Google Innovation	Google Mobile
Google+	Maps	Code	Products (delivery)
Blogger	Earth		Search
Hangouts	Panoramio		Maps
Groups			

Google Home and Office

G-mail, Drive, Docs, Sheets, Slides, Forms, Drawings, Sites, Calendar, Translate,
Google Cloud Print, Google Keep, Google Store

——————————————— Google search ———————————————

Breaking search speed records

Google wants to provide you with the quickest possible access to your end
result. In many areas of life it is often about the journey, rather than the
destination; however, in terms of delivering searchers to the destination best
matching their needs, it is solely about getting them to their destination as
speedily as possible.

This ties into the Google principle that 'faster is better than slow'. What
can be surprising with Google is the simplicity that is a constant thread
through every principle. The more you think about the notion of simplicity,
the more this becomes an increasing area of success within the company –
perhaps its greatest.

Speed of delivery brings us back to the first principle we discussed, 'Everything
stems from user focus'. Providing people with the fastest answers to questions,

and responses to queries, reflects the understanding that people's time is precious. The level of success that Google has had in improving speed and accuracy of delivery has shaped user demands and expectations of search experience from desktop to mobile search, plus everything else in between.

It is a huge achievement of Google to be able to deliver the vast majority of search results in fractions of a second (almost instantaneously). The end result of increasingly efficient search result delivery comes from constant refinement and innovation, as well as this commitment to 'doing search well'.

Votes count on the internet

Although Google has tested numerous approaches to deciding the ranking of websites for any given search query, it relies (certainly in no small part) on external trust signals to understand the value and relevancy of a web page and website for satisfying user demand. Here we are talking mainly about links.

A link from content on one website to content on another provides a direct association between information and a means for Google to crawl and discover (and index) new content. It is also possible for search engines like Google to identify numerically how many votes a website gathers as a signal of perceived external trust and authority on any particular topic. It is both quality and quantity that are present for this mathematical weighting based on votes of confidence.

There are hundreds of ranking factors that combine in the Google algorithm to deliver the end results that we experience in a fraction of a second. It is the expected value that can be derived from such things as external linking (tied to the widely recognized search and user value from backlinks) that has fuelled the growth of link building and associated areas.

As you would expect within any political voting system (assuming any opportunity for unfair play), the more inclusive the voting system is, and the broader the uptake of people participating in the vote, the fairer and more representative the final result will be. This is no different for search success in Google.

The following is a practical example of a situation where an 'example company' could generate external trust signals (in this example, links pointing to the website).

Company B sells a complex product which solves many problems, but is difficult for people to understand and therefore purchase. By creating some on site-linkable assets, the company has an opportunity naturally to pick up votes of confidence (ie links pointing to the site from external websites – also referred to as 'backlinks').

In this example, the linkable assets created include a video that explains the purpose of the product, some frequently asked questions answered on the site, and an infographic covering the main problems solved by this product.

In addition to the natural linking of external sites to this content (likely after some form of content promotion to get the information in front of the right people), there is a means to use that content to push out to the market for extra proactive link building. For example, searching social media for pertinent questions and then pointing people to the answers set out on the website, where this new content has been added.

Answers are everywhere

Wherever you are and whenever you want access to information, Google wants to be able to provide it for you. The growth of mobile emancipation worldwide combined with the ability for search results and internet content to be mobile friendly, means that delivery of information is no longer restricted to people sitting at their computer in a single location.

Progression in mobile technology empowers search engines to deliver a full alternative mobile search experience with ever limited differentiation (an almost like-for-like service) between mobile delivery compared to desktop.

You can be good and make money

Google is a profit-making entity. It needs to make money in order to succeed in any of the other goals the business has. When people apply human characterization to companies, they are very often showing negative (and even evil) characteristics. This is something Google is very keen to challenge and change.

Google makes profit from the search technologies and advertising they supply. To guide the delivery of approach Google has three pillars for adverts.

In Figure 2.5 you can see the three pillars for Google advertising. These are categorized as Relevancy, Simplicity and Integrity.

Discovery never stops

The growth of information is exponential. There is always a driving requirement to find more content, understand it and display it for the relevant search query. New information types are being created and accessed continuously and a key item of the Google guiding principles is this constant discovery and display of information.

FIGURE 2.5   The three principal pillars of Google advertising

Relevancy	Simplicity	Integrity
Not all search results have sponsored (paid for) advertising.	Advertising is not distracting users from the search results page.	All forms of paid advertising are clearly marked as such in the Google search results.
An important part of the logic behind this stems from the fact the adverts must be relevant, and therefore add some degree of value to the user.	They (sponsored ads) do not 'pop out', offer animation, or incorporate other 'flashy' distractions.	This enables the user to make informed decisions and differentiate between earned and paid results being provided.
Google believe that adverts can also offer worth to the user and although advertising is a primary revenue generator for the company, it will only be present if it fulfils the relevancy criteria.	Adverts are text based – this has proven to offer greatest click-through rates – something fundamental to the increasing success of the paid advertising media.	Google adhere to their own standards of integrity and objectivity when it comes to the ranking of paid-for positions in the sponsored sections of the search engine results pages.

Universal access to information

Regardless of age, demographic, geo location, or any other individual attributes, Google aims to be able to deliver access to the information you are looking for.

Google was founded in a single country (California in the United States), but that does not limit its global presence. This principle is a driving force for many (if not almost all) of the Google initiatives and innovations experienced over a number of years.

Google sets itself the challenge of providing a ubiquitous service that transcends physical barriers and it views as paramount the ideal that everybody should be able to access and enjoy the web (through Google).

Culture encourages creativity

Google is very public and proud of the fact that you do not need to adhere to historical business expectations to be successful. In fact, it strongly opposes many of these expectations as barriers to progress. The wearing of suits, always pursuing professional conduct, and the idea that fun (or play) belongs outside of office hours, could not be further from the truth in a Google office.

The Google ethos is something many companies do strive, or in my experience, certainly should strive towards. The following are some of the ingredients that support the culture Google has created.

Figure 2.6 shows the main ingredients required for creating the working life and broader culture at Google.

FIGURE 2.6   The recipe for creating life at Google

Life at Google

Ignoring the impossible
People make culture
Problem solving complexity with creativity
Diversity of intelligence and passion
An 'I do' attitude
Motivation to do what matters
Championing the largest challenges
Deepest data
Bigger, better, smarter
Creating your own career path
Making the difficult simple
Healthy mind, body and soul
Being 'a little different'
Speed of delivery regardless of role

SOURCE: (Google (2015) 'Life at Google' [Online] www.google.co.uk/about/careers/lifeatgoogle [Last accessed 07.11.2015]

Great is a good starting point

Google never settles for great. By setting unachievable goals, Google encourages the team to stretch, grow and deliver what doesn't exist – yet. Using an iterative approach to refinement, improvement and innovation, Google is always moving forward. When Google does something great for the many, the next Google logical step is to question why it is not providing something great for the remaining few.

An example of this in practice is the progression of Google towards artificial intelligence (AI). Without doubt, if a searcher knows what they are looking for, then in 99 per cent of cases, Google will give them what they need. So, when applying the Google logical next step, the question is 'how do we (Google) service the people who don't know what they are looking for?' – The answer is AI.

By understanding the context behind the query and constantly looking for the next gap to appear, Google can teach its robots/machines to learn, guess, improve and anticipate. This integration of the predictive stages of artificial intelligence supports the Google ethos of never settling for great and servicing the user beyond what they currently know they need.

The symbiotic nature of Google and SEO

In the first chapter of the book, we learnt more about what SEO is and why it matters. We took some time to understand how SEO plays an important role in servicing a number of basic business needs. We looked at some of the human attributes of SEO and discussed the value of earning results online.

So far, this chapter has focused on understanding more about Google – notably, the ethos behind the business. Whether you have a thorough understanding of Google and SEO, or your experience is based only on what you have read so far in this book, you will probably have noticed a few instances of similarity between SEO and Google.

From purpose, through to aims and aspirations, Google and SEO have a great deal of commonality, and this symbiotic relationship has existed as long as both have been in existence. The word 'symbiotic' describes the interdependent relationship that exists between the two. The following sections all focus on visible points of common cause and the mutual benefit derived from aligned aims and aspirations, using the Google principles as points of comparison.

It's all about the end user

In both Google and SEO, the end user is at the forefront of everything that is done. This is unlikely always to have been the case, as both are profit-making entities – so remuneration must have been the initial driving force for creation, at least to some extent. However, when looking at the successes achieved in this relationship, they are built on user value.

Search is everything

There is no conflict at all in this area of the relationship. A primary function of both SEO and Google is to increase visibility. Where the two differ comes down to impartiality. SEO is performed to assist a company achieve its online objectives, while Google maintains that it simply wants the best result to be returned. The approach for many SEO strategies to achieving visibility gains, will however, bring the two entities back in alignment. The reason for this is tied to providing the best result and helping Google find it.

Faster is better

Regardless of the method used to access websites, it is important that the speed of delivery (ie discovering the results in the first place and then loading them and delivering them to the user) is as efficient as possible. Google provides free tools for improving mobile and desktop site speed, and frequently a part of the SEO specialist role is making sure they are understood, applied, seen as important items for website health and in some cases set as benchmarks for improving.

Websites need links

Google constantly uses links to locate new content. Links are used for democratic value attribution and they enable algorithmic quality assessment. Links tell Google that a website has a physical location (among other signals) and encourage the passing of authority from one website to another. Every one of these link purpose items is required to support SEO success.

Google and SEO do not always cooperate when it comes to links (think of Google manual link penalties and negative algorithm impact from Google Penguin updates and the historical nature of link farms and spam link building for adding artificial value in SEO), but the nature of a symbiotic relationship is not always one of support and collaboration.

The ability of Google to identify low quality, spam and unwanted (or unnatural) linking has however, been fuelled, in no small part, by thousands of SEO expert man hours reviewing sites, redressing Google manual penalties and submitting disavow files (see below) to Google.

Visibility requires access

In nearly all instances, the purpose of optimizing is for content, web pages or websites to be seen and accessed – at any time, from any location and using any device. SEO and Google are certainly cooperating in this area and, while it is often the host (Google) that maps the journey, SEO is almost always the energy continually fuelling that journey, and the evangelist promoting it. When Google makes a statement regarding search updates and changes, SEO experts are almost always the first to ensure that this message is communicated expansively, incorporated into strategy and applied onto websites as a priority.

Working for the greater good

Yes, SEO and Google ultimately have a remit to make money, but both services provide a deeper value. From facilitating people's opportunity to have their voices heard, and the chance to compete in a more cash-neutral environment (there is never a completely cash-neutral environment), to identifying and fulfilling user search needs. The more thoroughly you delve into the motivations of SEO and Google, the more easily you are able to identify the common trend of working towards the greater good.

There's always a next action

Data never stops; neither does refinement of delivery, innovation or improvement. You could argue that SEO *has* to innovate to have any chance of success, but there is also an aspect of competition that would be present regardless of the search engine or marketing medium.

Creative thinking counts

Both Google and SEO are solving complex and interrelated problems – there are many areas of overlap – and a number of these relate back to anticipating user needs and helping people find the right content. While Google algorithms and searcher demands continue to grow, so too do the solutions needed to meet them.

Great is a starting point, not a final destination

Increasing competition and the mass of alternatives available leads us almost inevitably to the fact that services provided must continue to be better than any other alternatives. While the previous statement is more concentrated on SEO service provision, this constant improvement methodology absolutely applies to Google, regardless of its current worldwide monopoly.

Your SEO Google checklist

This book is focuses on understanding the reasoning behind the actions (or the *why* behind the *what*) and this checklist is no different. Every item listed in this checklist has been included based on publicly available information from Google.[3]

There are SEO checklists available online covering every year for the last decade or more, but when we are truly looking at the fundamentals of an SEO checklist for Google, this reference source, when supported by SEO best practice, is ideal for longer term relevancy. This is *not* an exhaustive SEO checklist of the granular items to complete within an SEO strategy;

rather it is specifically based on Google core optimization items which remain a constant for laying your SEO foundations to deliver longevity of search gains.

Figure 2.7 provides your fundamental checklist for optimizing for Google. Included in this checklist are core SEO expertise tasks including pre-click optimization (title tags and meta descriptions), website architecture, mixed content maximization, crawling, indexation and much more.

FIGURE 2.7   SEO checklist for Google optimization

The basics of SEO for Google

This section of the checklist concentrates on the basics required to support SEO success in Google. These areas have remained a consistent optimization foundation for a number of years and still provide distinct SEO value today.

- *Title tags.* Every page that you want to be visible online has a unique <title> tag. This tag gets added to the <head> section of the HTML page and accurately reflects the content contained within the page on which it is placed. Pixel lengths can be used accurately to incorporate characters into the restricted space of a title tag; however, if you restrict character lengths to 55 characters or fewer, this should ensure that title tags are not overly long, and that they display in full in the search engine results pages. In most cases (note – Google can choose alternative data to display in the title tag) the title tag you supply, will be the content that gets displayed in the Google search results organic advert for the respective page to which it has been added.

  Title tag tip: Inserting key terms in the title tag will support rankings gains. The sooner the key terms are placed in the title tag, the greater the potential emphasis and value derived from the tag to support specific SEO improvements.

- *Meta descriptions.* The supplemental information that sits below the title tag and forming the supporting role for your organic advert, the meta description summarizes the page/content for the user to make an informed decision to click. As seen with title tags, meta descriptions have a restricted amount of display space in Google. Again, you can use pixel lengths in order to maximize every pixel available for including copy in your meta descriptions, but using 155 characters or fewer will generally be a more efficient approach to meta description creation.

  Meta tag tip: Make sure that meta descriptions are reflective of the site content to encourage Google to use the data you provide, as opposed to alternative information lifted from the destination page. Remember to include calls to action, giving users a reason to 'Click Here!'. By adding to the meta description relevant content associated with the topic of the page you can encourage the bolding of text, should content in your meta description match the user search query. This can help the content stand out from surrounding and competing adverts in the organic search listings and potentially improve clicks from your adverts (click-through rates (CTR)).

Structuring your website

This part of the checklist looks at the website structural components that can facilitate easier site crawling and understanding for users and search engines

FIGURE 2.7 *Continued*

for your site. In line with the purpose of this checklist, these items have been ongoing optimization points for some time, and will provide value add opportunity for the foreseeable future.

- *Simple descriptive URLs.* Uniform Resource Locators (URLs) provide the address for referencing any resources on the internet. Keeping URLs user friendly and easy to read and search, as well as making them descriptive of the content contained within the URL, makes it easier for users to understand, share and ultimately click on your content and for search engines to crawl, categorize and display the content.

  URL tips: Remove any unwanted or excessive terms in URLs. Avoid using any characters other than standard alphabetical and numerical character sets. Look to include the most pertinent topic or theme for the page within URLs, but avoid repetition and keyword stuffing.

- *Website structure.* The way you organize your website's information hierarchy (put simply, the structure of the website) directly impacts the ease with which users and search engines can access your information. The priority order in which you place the content within your websites structure also provides direct signals to search engines on the perceived importance of content and how it fits into the site as whole. Easily accessible, prominently placed content will have a much greater claim for ranking gains than content buried under excessive layers of sub-folders or orphaned off (inaccessible) from the main navigation elements of the website. If you have a website that is dedicated to one core set of services, adding in completely unrelated content may make it difficult for that separate topic or focus area to succeed (note – there are a number of ways to redress this), as it can be a challenge to educate Google on how this alternative topic fits within the broader picture of the website.

  Site structure tip: Planning your site architecture and navigation is one of the most important steps – if not the most important – for creating a site for search success. Think about how people are expected to engage and interact with your website. The most common user journey starts on the home page of a website and this can be a great starting point for theorizing about and adding value to the user journey. Every level of the website needs to be thoroughly planned and reflective of the level of importance and priority placed on that content. As a general tip for creating a supportive website structure, the most important content needs to sit as high up (have as few folders before it) in the site hierarchy as possible. Put simply, the closer content is to the home page (root folder '/'), the easier it will be to access and able to rank for the topic it represents. Consider the 'flow' of content and the logical association between it and look (in most cases) to provide navigation in a text format (or as a text alternative), so that search engines and users (whether or not things like JavaScript or Flash capabilities) can always access the navigation information.

- *Breadcrumbs.* A breadcrumb can be defined as a fragment or connection within a chain of information used to describe a process leading to an end result. Breadcrumb navigation is a visual aid for users and search engines to see the process for moving from one page on a website through to the root domain (home page). This helps the user to visit any of the preceding steps in the website hierarchy (often with the purpose of directly accessing other topic-specific information required in order to gain a more comprehensive understanding of the information area) and to see how the content on the page they are visiting sits within the website structure.

▶

FIGURE 2.7 *Continued*

Breadcrumb navigation tip: The breadcrumb navigation can help the user to engage with your connected content and support end results (goal completions), from wherever they start their journey. Using breadcrumbs can help search engines place greater context into content (outside of single page focus) and associate information with other layers of content on your website, helping with correct indexation and easier site crawling. Google can use breadcrumb navigation that has been coded accordingly to display the breadcrumb component parts in the search engine results pages. Typically, breadcrumb navigation sits horizontally underneath the main navigation close to the top of the screen. (Although there is no rule requiring you to do this, users are more likely to expect its placement here.) Sometimes, however, you can see other implementation of this including at the base of pages.

- *Site maps*. There are two types of site maps. A site map for the user, which is a standard mapping of the main pages of your website, usually structured in a hierarchy of pages reflecting the main navigation, and a Sitemap for the search engines (an XML Sitemap). The purpose of both site maps is to assist with locating content. (Note the different spellings for user site maps and search engine Sitemaps.)

  Site map tip: When you build an on-page site map for the user, this can often be your last chance to redirect them to the part of the website they were looking for, but were unable to find through traditional website navigation. User site maps include links to the key content areas of your site, but they should also be written primarily for the user. If there is key content on your site that users engage with most, make sure that it is included in your user site map.

  XML Sitemap tip: Created for search engines (notably Google) to find all of the content on your site that you wish to be crawled and indexed, Google provide Sitemap generator tools, the location to submit your Sitemap to (and update it frequently) as well as supportive tools for testing the XML Sitemap functions as expected. The way in which you include URLs in your Sitemap can also provide Google with direct signals (note – they may not always choose to adhere to these signals) of the correct version of a URL on your website (if you have multiple versions of pages accessible).

  General site maps tip: Site maps (user and XML versions) need to be kept updated. There are many areas on websites that require frequent updates for 'good housekeeping' and to encourage general website health. When you add new content to your website this should be reflected in both versions of site maps and there are a number of CMS plug-ins that can help you in this area by auto updating when new content is created. It is important that you have access to full control over any plug-ins however, as you want the correct versions of pages to be indexed and only *one* version of pages to be indexed, otherwise you can create problems that will require fixing.

- *Page not found (404)*. At some stage in the lifespan of your website you will have broken pages on your site. These crop up when you restructure content, remove old or dead pages or simply (as is the case for many CMS) update or change URLs over the lifespan of content. It is a natural occurrence of a website to have missing or broken content and what matters is how you prepare for, and deal with this when it occurs. A website should have a custom 404 page. This page has a header status of 404 (hence the page and broken page reference to 404 'page not found') providing a message from the server that content in not accessible on this specified URL.

  Page not found tip: By providing the correct header status code you can help prevent unwanted indexing of this page – remember that although the

FIGURE 2.7   *Continued*

page does offer search engine value, its primary function is to help the user. A 404 page should be considered as a final chance to redirect the user to important content on your website before they bounce to alternative search results content. A 404 page can showcase your most enjoyed, most relevant and most successful content for converting and engaging with users. Many sites like to get creative when it comes to 404 pages and show a more personal touch to content delivery outside of standard house style; however, remember that people landing on this page have already had barriers put in place between their search request and discovering the content they originally looked for, so effective access to core page and content on your site will in most cases be a preferable option.

Provision of quality content and service offerings

As you would expect from everything that has been discussed in this textbook up to this point, bringing user needs to the forefront of service and content provision is imperative. One of the obvious ways to service this requirement, that is fundamental to Google and search principals, is through visible and aspirational approaches in this area or performance. Most points on this checklist are very specific; however, areas such as 'quality' are often unique to your company and as such, some of these items in this section require more creative implementation. As with every section, however, tips have been included for practical progression on every item of your SEO checklist.

- *Creating buzz.* When you deliver something that is different, new and adds value to your audience, or simply offers a unique proposition or opinion, it is likely that this will encourage *noise* around your content. This can be people sharing and syndicating the content, talking about it in forums or other external websites, and very likely, people engaging directly with the content. The more buzz that you can create, the greater chance that this content will not only start to attract success, but also support search ranking gains.

  Creating buzz tip: Regardless of how great your content may be, people need to be able to discover it in the first place. Whenever adding and creating new content, ensure that your site has the technical capability to support the success of the content. Pages need to load quickly, provide the right search and user topical and structural signals and enable (as well as encourage) people to share it.

- *Anticipating user needs.* There is a wealth of data available about your audience: who they are; what their needs are; their search behaviour trends; seasonal and demographic demands; search query behaviour; mobile and cross-device search needs and so much more. All of this information can, and should be used to anticipate user needs and, more importantly, to fulfil them.

  Anticipating user needs tip: There is not a single approach to maximizing user needs through successful anticipation, but informing your decisions in this area with data, needs to be at the heart of this. Creativity plays an important role here too. There are also many systematic approaches that can be employed in this area of delivery. Think about things such as mixed content types, and depth of information provided. This will offer search vertical specific gains (images, video, news, blogs etc) as well as the ability to target people at various stages of the information seeking and buying process. In addition to this, people digest information differently, so applying a more diverse mix of content types will help to service a greater volume of expected (anticipated) user needs.

  Quick content tips: Because content is so important to the success of SEO and forms *the* interaction between a site and its users in every aspect

▶

FIGURE 2.7   *Continued*

of delivery, the topic itself is vast. The following are a few quick tips for creating content that works online. Use correct spelling and grammar. Provide structure to the content, helping people read it effectively regardless of device. Provide a clear topic focus and access to a greater depth of content if the user should want to immerse themselves in that topic. Give the user instructions on what they are expected to do next, rather than leaving them to figure this out for themselves. Ensure that content is accessible to all users and on all browsers and devices. Make sure that content has been created with a purpose (and that purpose should not be search engine rankings). Ensure content is unique, has a perspective and provides something new to the audience digesting it.

- *Anchor text.* This is text that is clickable within links. Anchor text provides users and search engines with information about the destination of the link.
  Anchor text tip: The more descriptive the anchor text is the better. Try to avoid excessive use of phrases like 'read more', 'click here' and other generic calls to action. Make sure that anchor text is written for the user. Despite the fact that anchor text is a ranking factor and that keywords are still important in this area of optimization, the goal is for the user to click on the link and for search engines to understand the context and meaning of the link. Keep anchor text short and make sure it is unique in most instances. Anchor text is not just for external links – it is for *all* links – and again, there is direct value in effectively optimizing anchor text (both for the user and for search engines).

- *Images.* All distinct types of content have very specific optimization opportunities over and above that of 'general' content optimization.
  Image tip: Images should have descriptive file names, as this will help search engines understand and index the content effectively and can support ranking gains. It can be useful to store all images in the same folder, as this simplifies access. Stick to the more common image file types, so that you can be confident that they will be supported across all browser types. Ensure that all images have alt text (the alt attribute) included. Alt text displays if the image file does not render correctly (broken links, non-supported browsers etc) and provides a description of the image for screen readers and other accessibility tools. Consider the surrounding content close to the image as well as other on-page theme items, as these can all support better image indexation and context. Having a separate XML Sitemap for images, will support greater image search value, speedier crawling and indexation and more.

- *Headers.* Header tags (eg <h1>, <h2>, <h3> etc) provide structure to the content – there are six levels of header tags (h1–h6), with the level of importance starting at h1 and reducing down to h6. With CSS styling they enable easier content digestion and the ability to skim read content quicker. Headers also give search engines very specific information about the page theme as well as core components of the page content.
  Header tip: In most instances (HTML5 can be exceptions), a page will have a single h1 tag; this identifies the primary topic or theme of the page. Pages with any depth of content will have a number of supporting (sub) headers. Think about how the page will look with only headers in place – does that picture reflect the content and give you a solid understanding of the core content areas? If not, you will need to reconsider the use of headers for a more effective outcome.

FIGURE 2.7 *Continued*

Website crawling

An action completed by Google bots, crawling of content is the initial action required in order for fresh content to be found and indexed so that it then has the potential to be displayed for matching user search queries.

- *Robots.txt.* A robots.txt file is a simple text document added to the root folder of your domain (eg testsite.com/robots.txt) and enables you to provide instructions for search engines on content (specific pages, files or entire sections of a website (and in some cases the whole site)) that you *do not* want to be crawled or indexed.

  Robots.txt tip: Most websites will have content included on them that is not for the user to see. This can include logged in or private pages, duplicate content, forms and more. A number of content management systems (CMS) also create pages, filters and other site folders and content that you will not want to be accessible or promoted online. You can also use on-page 'noindex' and 'nofollow' instructions to search engines to supply signals of pages where the intention is not to have content followed or not to have content indexed (or both). An example of this code (in this case for instructing Google not to follow the content) is <meta name='robots' content='nofollow'>.

- *Rel='nofollow'.* Part of crawling also includes external content pointing authority to your site's content. With any spam links, unwanted links or irrelevant linking anchors, you will want to have the rel='nofollow' attribute added to the links. This tells crawlers not to follow the link, crawl the content or pass on any value (from the reputation of the linking site) to the corresponding content that it links to.

  Rel='nofollow' tip: An important part of website 'good housekeeping' is regular link (notably backlink) reviews. From low-quality scraping sites and irrelevant directories, right through to irrelevant content, handling unwanted linking is something that needs ongoing and proactive attention.

Mobile optimization

The growth of mobile devices and the mission of universal access to answers anywhere, any time and on any device, means that site must to be mobile ready. This includes mobile friendliness, mobile usability and more.

- *Mobile friendly.* A website is mobile friendly when the site in its entirety performs to a high standard on mobile devices regardless of screen size or user intention when visiting your site using a mobile device.

  Mobile-friendly tip: Google provides a mobile-friendly test, use this for any URL to see specific pass or fail updates needed to make your site mobile friendly (and likely perform more successfully in mobile search results). A site is mobile friendly if it uses content types available on mobile devices (ie not using flash), has readable text without the need for zooming in, it sizes content to fit varying screen sizes without user actions and places content that is spaced, enabling users to tap content effectively.

- *Site speed.* For both mobile and desktop, site speed directly impacts rankings as well as the ability for content to be crawled and indexed by search engines, and actually read by end users. The quicker content loads, the better for search in general, but this is especially the case with mobile devices.

  Site speed tip: There are lots of free tools available online for site-speed improvements, including page speed tools provided by Google – these will give you site wide and page specific implementation items to improve site speed. It is a good idea to prioritize mobile actions based on the potential positive impact for the user and for total speed performance. There are always quick wins in site-speed updates and this can be a great way to add value and to encourage site-wide success online.

Why other search engines matter

Google may account for 65, 75 or more than 85 per cent of your total organic (or SEO) website traffic. This rightly demands a focus on Google as a key search strategy tied to a desired return on that attention. It is not uncommon that when people mention search engine optimization, they conflate SEO with Google – think about statements like 'Googling it now' and 'I will just Google that'.

This type of learnt behaviour transcends a single search engine, even though it implies only one option for searching. The fact is, there are many alternatives to Google and they can all provide value to your SEO results.

Part of this (single search engine focus) is certainly true in many strategies (even more prolific in restricted SEO resource environments) and in part, leads us back to the symbiotic relationship between Google and SEO. A part is also unfounded and this needs to be redressed.

Every search engine (and there are lots of them in addition to the handful that you may have heard about) offers a unique opportunity to reach a new target audience and to take advantage of the nuances of the search engine itself. From a holistic point of view, having all of your focus on a single search engine is a risky strategy, as although it would be extremely difficult to replace Google (notably in English search results where it is so dominant), diversification offers some protection should you find penalties or negative algorithm impact impedes your sites success in Google.

Bing, for example, the Microsoft search engine, is usually the main challenger to Google in terms of market share – even more so in the United States than in the United Kingdom. Known for its striking background image on load of the homepage, Bing also provides a means directly to compare Bing and Google results delivered through **www.bingiton.com**.

Yahoo is often seen as a more focused provider of news and media search vertical results. Yahoo offers so many other supportive tools and user options directly from the search engine, that people often consider it as more of a toolkit, as opposed to solely being a search engine. When you think about solution-driven search potential Yahoo Answers is a fantastic opportunity to generate specific search gains outside of the traditional SERP marketing model.

YouTube (even though owned by Google) gives you the opportunity to tap into video search in isolation. Video content is great for problem solving and 'how to' type search gains. The speed of video creation and the value of mixed content types (as well as the disparate target audience compared to that of traditional text content) provides many reach opportunities extending that of search engine results pages.

Product search engines like Amazon enable online shops to have specific presence based on the dominance of these e-commerce giants online. As these *product search engines* are targeting more informed searchers often nearing the final stages of information seeking and buying behaviour, they aim to match product search queries to product suppliers.

Micro blogging search engines (Twitter being at the fore in this field) offer access to trends, reach, engagement and general speedy interaction between people, brands, news, media and more, through a unique framework, appealing to audiences outside and in addition to, the Google model.

Ask (previously Ask Jeeves) has the appeal of offering a more personalized approach to communication based on asking a question and having 'Jeeves' reply with relevant ranges of answers. The range of answers provided and the supplemental options for further discovery on the information-finding journey can make Ask a viable option for targeted marketing and depth of topic and direct question-and-answer content delivery.

Key terms

Definitions have been included below to support a thorough overview of the more industry-derived and niche terminology used throughout this chapter. For ease of reference, all of the definitions are listed in the order that they first appear in this chapter.

Googleplex

This is Google's name for its company head office.

ethos (Google)

The characteristics that underlie the culture of the company. This reflects the promoted spirit of the Google community: the beliefs, attitudes, practices and culture which can be used to define the business.

manifesto

Traditionally associated with political parties or individuals, in this context, it relates to the publicly available and company-declared information with regard to policies, aims and ambitions.

Google Doodle

There is a history of Google Doodles available directly online from Google at **www.google.com/doodles**. These fun and often interactive aspects of the Google search result pages reflect the only real distraction from the adverts (organic and paid), and supply value to the end user exceeding that of query resolution. The first Google Doodle appeared back in 1998 when Google founders Larry and Sergey wanted to advise users of their attendance at the 'Burning Man' festival in Nevada. Since this time they have covered everything from lunar events, right through to religious festivities.

Knowledge Graph

In 2012, Google launched the Knowledge Graph. The intention of this update to the Google search results displayed was to provide the user with direct (pre-click) information relating to their original search request. Primarily targeted to facts about places, people and entities, the role of the Knowledge Graph is to show how these topics are connected. As an example, if you type into Google famous footballer, England and Tottenham striker, 'Harry Kane', the Knowledge Graph will provide you with [last access date 31-10-2015] Harry Kane's bio snippet from Wikipedia, recent images from football matches he has been involved in, his social media profiles, height, weight, date of birth (and myriad other publicly available personal details), plus other footballers based on 'People also search for' machine learning.

carousel

In 2013, Google provided an alternative display style (a top of the search engine results carousel style of content) for a number of local listings relating to search areas, including leisure queries for hotels and eating out. This carousel replaced the traditional vertical search listings (ie the Local Pack) when the number of local listings in the pack apparently exceeded five listings. One of the potential benefits with this delivery of greater quantities of local listings horizontally rather than vertically, is the reduction of the potential negative impact of not being top of the local pack (the click-through rate nearly always proportionately declines with vertical position drop). Another potential benefit with the carousel functionality for Local Pack results is the diversity of the remainder of the SERP for deeper results delivery and diversity of information returned (over sometimes excessive local dominance).

Local Pack

Traditionally, Google has displayed a variety of Local Pack results, starting from a set of seven results (with a Google map preceding the text results) and varying towards a three results pack with a 'read more' functionality to click to see extra local results. When people are searching for queries tied to location (eg dining out, hotels or other services), it is assumed that location relevancy will be a key factor for user context and intent.

democratic

Traditionally relating to forms of government, in this context the concept is tied to the idea that the delivery of search results incorporates some degree of fair representation of the internet community, through the inclusion of user votes (in the form of choosing to link to external content) within the Google search algorithm.

algorithm

Notably in relation to computers, an algorithm is a defined process and guiding set of rules that can be followed without change in order to deliver a consistent way of solving problems.

universal

Applying to everyone – all-inclusive. This refers to removing any exclusions or exceptions.

geo location

In the intended use of the term within this chapter, geo location refers to the physical location of people, devices and entities.

demographic

Here we have used this as a means of covering types of segmentation. Demographics relates to the study of specific types of information such as age, sex, nationality and so on.

artificial intelligence

The ability for machines to *learn* in order to take on some of the roles, responsibilities and work that normally require human intelligence.

symbiosis

The process of two entities working/living together, with some form of co-dependence.

Google Penguin

A filter applied to Google search engine results pages (SERPs) to access the positive or negative value of a website focusing on link profiles. A low-quality (spam, unnatural or over optimized) link profile can be seen as questionable by Google Penguin and result in a negative (or lesser reported, positive) impact on the ability of individual pages, sections or entire websites to perform (ie rank highly on the most important visibility areas for that website) online.

disavow file (Google)

By using the Google disavow tool (ie a graphical user interface that enables webmasters to upload a single disavow file numerous times), a webmaster can notify Google of unwanted external links pointing to the website. As most links pointing to a website are not within the control of the website owner/manager (ie they site on external domains that the website to which they are linking does not have access in order to make website updates themselves), it is necessary to be able to remove any association from them, notably when looking to complete website *housekeeping* or removing algorithm negative impact or manual link penalties.

key points

- Google dominates global search. The percentage of market share of Google is more than three times that of its nearest competition in the United States.
- The Google manifesto entitled the 'Ten things we know to be true' is directly relevant to search engine success.
- From purpose through to aims and aspirations, Google and SEO have a great deal of commonality which can be used to drive winning search strategies.
- By understanding Google, you can create specific Google/SEO checklist items. These have been consistent optimization areas

historically, and will continue to form core Google search strategy for the foreseeable future.

- Despite Google's search dominance, there are many alternative search engines to Google and they can all provide value to your SEO results.

Notes

1 comScore qSearch (2015) 'comScorereleases March 2015 US desktop search engine rankings' [Online], https://www.comscore.com/Insights/Market-Rankings/comScore-Releases-March-2015-US-Desktop-Search-Engine-Rankings [Last accessed 28.10.2015])

2 Google Company (2015) 'Ten things we know to be true' [Online], https://www.google.co.uk/about/company/philosophy/ [Last accessed 28.10.2015]

3 Google (2010) 'Search Engine Optimization Starter Guide' [Online], http://static.googleusercontent.com/media/www.google.com/en//webmasters/docs/search-engine-optimization-starter-guide.pdf [Last accessed 09.11.2015]

The restraints of process-driven SEO and the value of opportunity

03

LEARNING OUTCOMES

In this chapter we look at the limitations of adhering to strict processes when it comes to search engine optimization, implementing search strategy and making the most of opportunities for online results. After reading this chapter you will be better able to:

- understand the restraints of process-driven SEO

- understand and implement organic search marketing

- identify, amplify and implement opportunities

Every approach to SEO delivery will have some form of process. There is nothing wrong with including an element of process in SEO strategy. Indeed, without a clear framework and supporting processes your successes will not be repeatable; any failures will not become avoidable; and every project will be susceptible to gaps in service provision. Processes help mitigate inconsistencies, support strategic delivery, and encourage the application of expertise spanning the most important aspects of the medium.

This may lead us to ask the question: *So what is wrong with process-driven SEO?* A process should not define an approach to service delivery. Processes are insular by nature and rely on a repeated set of actions for a repeated and expected outcome. However refined a process may appear to be, it will always get to a stage where it becomes counterproductive and stifling of expertise and innovation.

SEO, while incorporating many 'knowns' (see Chapter 2 for a good checklist approach to optimizing for Google) also has a myriad of changeable variants which require flexibility, adaptation and creativity.

Understanding the restraints of process-driven SEO

What is a typical process?

Before we look at the constraints of a process, it is important that you can see the creation of a solid process for delivering SEO. We can then look at the attractions of following this process, and discuss the limitations of doing so.

- *Analysis*. Analysis may be a logical starting point for an SEO project. This should take full account of the current situation. At this stage you will want to benchmark every applicable key performance

FIGURE 3.1   A process for search engine optimization

indicator (KPI) and set the initial goals, objectives and deliverables. Analysis needs to be comprehensive as it sets the scene, determines expectations and fuels research. You should analyse not only the website's current performance in terms of search success, but also the website itself, the competition, the external environment, the historical performance of the site, and many other factors.

- *Research.* Through your data and situational analysis you will have taken note of strengths, weaknesses, opportunities and threats (traditional SWOT analysis) – all of which require further research, analysis and, ultimately, strategy creation. Research in this sense should be targeted investigation driven by data analysis.

- *Strategy.* By definition, a strategy is a plan to achieve a goal. Therefore, every strategy (whether a short-term micro strategy, or a longer term macro strategy, or something else in-between) will be targeted to an objective, and while SEO has some clear objectives as a service, customer objectives will always be unique in some way.

- *Technical.* Technical SEO really refers to the effectiveness of a website for enabling search engines to discover, crawl, index and, to some extent, understand your content (web page or website). Covering code, site structure, site speed, technical housekeeping and much more, it would be uncommon not to have a technical focal point for any SEO strategy.

- *On site.* On-site SEO focuses very much on content. By content we are really referring to every touchpoint of the website that interacts with a person or a search engine. On-site SEO includes every item located on the domain itself, including the domain name. On site also refers to items controlled on the website, even if they are visible externally. Good examples of this are meta descriptions and title tags – both controlled on site (usually via a CMS or traditional FTP), but seen off site.

- *Off site.* Search engine success relies largely on a combination of on-site and off-site website signals. Traditionally, off-site SEO is dominated by links; however, social PR, citations, brand value and other performance areas, not under the control of the physical website, all contribute to external authority gained and cumulative search success.

- *Report.* The reporting stage of a search strategy is necessary for identifying any progress made, gaps within the approach delivered and more importantly, proposed next actions required to work towards objective achievement. Report structures will vary, but it is useful to include coverage of the focus of the project, key metrics relating to any goals and objectives, actions completed to deliver potential gains, plus next steps to maintain progress on the project undertaken.

- *Refine.* You should not be working on single-point strategies with the delivery of SEO. Every action you complete provides new data sets and information from which you can directly impact the next actions you undertake. If you fail to use this changing information for supporting greater wins you will massively limit the performance of your search marketing campaigns.

Restraints of process-driven SEO

The process we looked at in the previous section enables you to analyse the situation, research the market, develop initial strategy, apply some key SEO tactics and refine your approach.

This is all very logical and there is no issue with following a process like this when you want to use clear points of reference to improve and apply an online strategy, or are seeking a very consistent method of applying SEO. There are, however, a number of restraints that come with following this or any other process, and it is important that you recognize this before embarking on process-driven SEO.

- *Tied to an approach.* When you follow a cyclical process, such as the one provided in the previous section, you are ignoring almost everything else that can have a dramatic impact on your search strategy and performance. The same can be said for any other process-driven strategy. The speed at which the SEO industry changes, combined with the pace of change in most business sectors, along with constantly increasing user demands (especially online), means that ignoring opportunities outside of your strategy will be a risky approach.

- *Following not leading.* When you make the decision to follow a set approach, however refined the strategy may be, you are making a choice to settle for the limitations of that strategy as it stands today. Consider Google's principles that we discussed in Chapter 2, and the success derived from constant innovation and refinement. This type of success could never be achieved through heavy process.

- *Stifling creativity.* Think about the most creative people you know. How many of those same people impose stringent structure or process on their approach to work or associated scenarios? Take a moment to consider the best digital marketing campaigns you remember from childhood and attempt to reverse engineer the thought process behind the lightbulb moment that led to the inception of the strategy. For many of the great search and digital marketing successes, you need the fundamentals of expertise, you need the right people in the room, and you need to create a safe environment where people can have big ideas regardless of any processes in place. Excessive reliance on structure is one of the biggest limitations on creative success – so it should be avoided.

- *Reacting to impact.* Because process-heavy SEO focuses on the thorough delivery of a set of known processes, most of the attention relates to the process itself and the accurate implementation the process. While this gives you a repeatable means to service your interpretation of SEO, it does not allow you proactively to create positive impact or negate potential negative impact. The industry will not wait for you to complete your research phase of strategy prior to rolling out a link-based penalty. A competitor will not hold back their launch of a new innovative product series for you to finish your off-page tactics. These are just a couple of examples of how reacting to impact will become a negative factor for process following.

- *Experts want to make an impact.* The level of expertise within the SEO industry and digital environment in general is phenomenal. One of the most satisfying parts of the job is being able to make a positive difference. People who have spent years formulating a deeper understanding of the industry will have skill sets developed from a unique set of circumstances and experiences far beyond that of a process created, however complex and revisited that process may have become. Gut feeling should not be a basis for decision making; but culture, ideas, creativity, interpretation, experience, testing, innovation and so much more should be core refinement criteria for search engine optimization.

- *Complacent thinking reduces results.* If you ask a question about the logic behind decision making and the answer is something along the lines of 'that's the way we've always done it', you are likely to be working in an excessively process-driven culture, and possibly need to reflect on the *real* logic behind the approach. Doing something because at some stage (who knows how long ago, or the reason why), someone added it to a process, should not lead to that process being blindly followed for the indefinite future. When you start to settle for the status quo you breed a culture that supports complacency, and this is something that cannot be allowed in an increasingly competitive search environment.

- *Avoiding risks reduces robustness.* It seems perfectly natural to avoid risks; in many areas of everyday life this is absolutely essential. In a business sense, however, you sometimes have to take calculated risks or you may start to become ineffective. Experimentation, trialling of new ideas and challenging the 'norm' are all prerequisites for a robust, innovative and industry-leading service.

Understanding and implementing organic search marketing

Implementing effective, repeatable, and best practice organic search engine marketing (SEM) requires depth of understanding. You can *toe dip* into SEO delivery with basic coding or CMS knowledge, and some form of SEO guidance. However, as with any form of expert service delivery, it is very easy to waste resources and negatively impact a website's performance in search than it is to have a positive effect. The challenge becomes incrementally harder when you are striving for continuous results over a number of years (ie longevity of performance).

Already, in the earlier chapters of the book, you will have come across the phrase 'the *why* behind the *what*'. This is discussed in more detail now. As we look through some of the most successful SEO strategies and implementation areas, we will look at why deeper understanding is imperative for long-term SEO achievement. There follow just a few examples to reinforce this principle, but many others exist:

Creating industry-leading content

Good content is not enough if you are competing in even, low to medium competitive online markets. Content must substantially improve upon the very best competing examples that you can discover online. With new websites entering into almost, every niche, most days, any content you create needs to support company differentiation, earn links and fuel social PR.

Content needs to have clear, identifiable value, not only relevant to the end goals you are looking for, but also covering the most comprehensive and varied needs of your current, and future target audiences.

Fine tuning your website

Most touchpoints for SEO strategy will be on, and interacting with, your website. A high-performing website requires constant monitoring and reaction to change. The website should be live and available (not experiencing down-time), so that is can be used 24/7 and crawled at any time of the day, or day of the week, 365 days of the year, every year. Sites need to be accessible on every device, every location, and provide a seamless user experience from the very first click on a search result, through to every interaction thereafter.

Like cars, websites need frequent servicing, parts replacing, performance refined and sometimes full restoration or even replacement. The decision to repair or replace is usually driven by changing needs of the people who use the car most of the time – and the same can often be said for websites.

Doing the basics brilliantly

In this sense 'the basics' are specific actions that should be in place, reviewed frequently, and be present in almost every SEO campaign. When things change (new content gets added to a website, a site changes domain etc) these basic tasks require complete review and updating. A few examples of the basics include: theming a page so that it has a distinct topic; ensuring content has effective structure; creating an optimized website structure; adhering to Google guidelines; creating a content hierarchy; and making it easy for content to be shared and digested.

Expanding your search horizons

Many SEO projects are less effective at delivering results than they should be, due in no small part to their limited scope. While it is important to have clear objectives and desired end results, this should not restrict the need to think big and aim for everything. One of the most obvious ways in which self-imposed limitations manifest themselves is with keywords. Historically, the SEO industry has focused very much on single keywords. Every website would have a clear set of hero terms, and the success of the service would be largely associated with the progress made in moving these single terms (small term groupings) higher up in the search engine results pages. When you focus on 20 or 30 words, you miss out on thousands (if not hundreds of thousands) of others. These restrictions exist in many areas in SEO delivery. This is just one area in which you can expand your horizons.

Providing a good experience

Because experience can be subjective and personal, getting user experience right is never a one-off exercise, and needs a lot of split testing and ongoing data work to encourage continuous improvements. As devices change and technology evolves, you will find the demands of user experience also increase as expectations are raised. It would be surprising to see the effective lifespan of a website exceed 24 months (assuming starting from a complete overhaul) and provide a user experience anywhere near its potential.

Building relationships

Search engines do not work without link signals. There are lots of types of digital relationships and most of them include linking in one form or another. Links help search engines find, crawl and index content. They also provide an external vote of confidence and a passing of authority from one website to another. A link can be contained within a single domain and point externally to many other domains. Links can have a positive effect on performance or lead towards penalization of a website by infringing on Google guidelines. Successful digital relationships offer value outside of performance enhancement, and have a positive impact on the respective audiences on both sides of the relationship (and likely on the wider search industry).

Identifying, amplifying and implementing opportunity

The vast majority of search opportunities go unrealized. It is the untapped opportunity that empowers expert search marketers to deliver incremental website gains and encourage a continuous improvement approach to websites, users and search engine optimization.

When you discover an opportunity you need to be able to amplify it and implement it effectively to achieve the greatest potential end results.

FIGURE 3.2   Your identification tree for discovering opportunity in search data

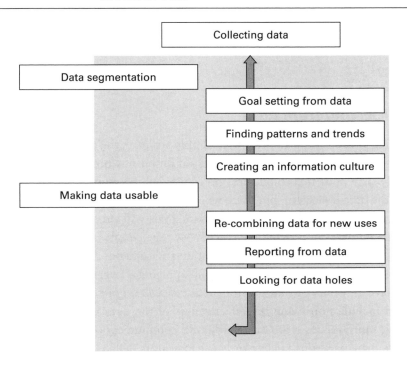

Collecting data

The first stage in search opportunity is data collation. Many companies will have a number of current data sets available to them, and pulling this data into a manageable database will make identifying, amplifying and implementing opportunity much more effective. The more comprehensive your data set becomes the more value you will be able to get from it. There is a point at which data can become unmanageable (usually due to the volumes of data to which people have access) and at this stage you need to start segmenting what you have.

Data segmentation

Gathering data will help to identify new opportunities, actionable insights (by knowing more about the opportunity), as well as information to make more of what is already in place (amplification). At this stage you will be able to consider what segments of the data are delivering the most initial value, and how deeper elements of the data (or database) can become more visible to spot hidden opportunities. When segmenting, data do not focus *only* on the data currently returning value, as realistically, most opportunities will not be available until it is better segmented. A large part of the user base completing actions from the data will only be aware of the shallow value it has tied to specific requirements of their role. Broadening this is an important data goal.

Goal setting from data

Defining goals is important for most ambitious projects; and receiving maximum value from big data is certainly an ambitious project. A number of data goals will be tied to business objectives (eg the number of conversions from the data collected), but there will be many indirect or non-commercial data goals too. As you might expect, data goals will vary greatly. One common data goal is improving the efficiency of the people using that data. For example, if a team takes 15 hours to set up and send out a regular marketing communication, segmenting the data and applying a level of data automation may save 14 hours of that previous *manual data labour.* Another data goal would include improving the effectiveness of the data used – in this case, getting more replies from any marketing communication sent, or perhaps other e-mail marketing key performance indicators (KPIs) including increasing open rates.

Finding patterns and trends

You will be surprised how quickly you and your team will start discovering new patterns and trends as soon as you create a more thorough set of data. Once you have segmented information, this facilitates easier data use and leads to opportunities that would previously have been buried. To find trends, you need to be actively looking for them. It is important to stop focusing on a single value or outcome from any data, and start considering what the data *does not* provide. This culture will evolve your data sets from the user up and from the business down. This relationship is needed to maximize opportunity and focus.

Creating an information culture

Not every person who uses data needs to have traditional data science or website analytical skills. In fact, you are likely to get more value out of the data by having a diverse set of people interacting with it. An information culture is one where people are working with data, understanding the data goals, and will not settle for any current data limitations.

Making data usable

Although data has an intrinsic value, the business will receive very restricted gains from information if it is not positioned in a way that is suited to the different groups of people using it. The vast majority of those who are expected to use the data will not need to understand where it comes from, or all of the stages it has passed through before it gets to them. However you decide to provide the data, you will need to minimize anything the end user has to do before the data becomes useful and useable for them.

Re-combining data for new uses

When you present data to users you are giving them a very clear (and deliberately restricted) view of the total data and how they can use it to provide opportunities (identifying, amplifying and implementation). The different data views remove the problem of excessive data and time wastage in getting to the stage where the data becomes useful and also provides the chances of ongoing data recombination. Users re-combining information for new uses is one of the most exciting gains delivered from successfully making data usable and building an information culture.

Reporting from data

An end result from data needs to include some form of reporting. Whether internal or external, reporting confirms that the data is working, details success of the data in achieving the goals set, and reinforces how the data needs to evolve. You will never have a complete data set, but you can continue to refine your data and report on the success that it delivers. Reporting is a necessary step for ongoing data funding and expansion, as well as augmenting the cumulative worth of the data.

Looking for data holes

Before the data collation begins again, you have to be looking for data gaps. A large aspect of this brings us back to establishing a data culture and re-combining data for new purposes; but this can also be aligned to individuals' roles in the company and a more formal approach to data.

Key terms

As with every chapter in this textbook, key terms and phrases have been defined below to assist with depth of learning and understanding. For ease of reference, all of the definitions are listed in the order that they first appear in this chapter.

Micro strategy

In its intended use in this chapter, a micro strategy is one that delivers a necessary step on the way towards a broader strategic achievement. For example, if you are a recruitment company and your overarching strategy (or macro strategy) is focused on people signing up for your service, a micro strategy could include tactics that lead to completion of steps such as completing a CV, submitting personal details and setting up a profile page.

Macro strategy

This is the broader strategy that looks to deliver your final goals. In the previous example this would be the collection of micro strategies, and anything in addition, required to get people to sign up to your service.

Technical SEO

This directly relates to Search Engine Optimization tactics required for a website to improve the ability for search engines to discover, crawl, index and, to some extent, understand your content (web page or website).

Meta description

An HTML attribute that provides the brief synopsis of a page's content that usually displays in the search engine results pages. By providing a meta description, you are advising the search engines of the preferred content that you would like to form part of your advert online.

Title tag

A required element for HTML pages, the title tag defines the title of the content (HTML document) it relates to. Also displaying in the search engine results pages, the title tag precedes the meta description and forms the title of your search advert.

FTP (File Transfer Protocol)

This is the term used to describe the transfer of computer files across the internet from one host to another.

Key points

- Every approach to SEO delivery will have some form of process. There is nothing wrong with including an element of process in SEO strategy; in fact, without a clear framework and supporting processes your successes will not be repeatable.

- A process should not define an approach to service delivery. Processes are insular by nature and rely on a repeated set of actions for a repeated and expected outcome.

- Implementing effective, repeatable, and best practice organic search engine marketing (SEM) requires depth of understanding.

- The vast majority of search opportunities go unrealized. It is the untapped opportunity that empowers expert search marketers to deliver incremental website gains and encourage a continuous improvement approach to websites, users and search engine optimization.

Supporting longevity with search ripples

LEARNING OUTCOMES

This chapter looks at longer and shorter term approaches to SEO delivery. We introduce the unique theory of 'ripples in search' and provide a practical way to use ripple theory in future SEO strategies that you create. Once you have read this chapter, you should have a better understanding of:

- long-term vs short-term mentality in search

- what ripples mean, and an introduction to new search ripple theory

- practical examples of ripple creation for your future search strategies

Long-term vs short-term mentality

This heading reflects the dilemma that many people face when completing any initial SEO strategy. One of the first challenges that an SEO expert regularly needs to overcome is getting the right balance between long-term and short-term approaches to search engine optimization. Often it is not a case of one option or the other, but a hybrid approach that combines varying degrees of both.

Long-term mentality

In previous chapters, we have discussed some of the fundamentals in search and many of the items have remained constant in potential value and in their application. A number of these are also pertinent to longer term approaches to SEO delivery. When we focus on longer term tactics, the inclusion criteria include the multiple use of the tactic for gains, extending the strategy application over the longer term.

For the rationale in this chapter, *long term* refers to a tactic that exceeds six months in a search engine marketing strategy, although the term will vary from situation to situation.

FIGURE 4.1   Long-term mentality tactics timeline (day one to day 'n')

Website – build and maintenance	Content – user and search servicing	User – interaction and value	Location – building and expanding	Search – fulfilment and opportunity	Verticals – identifying and maximizing

Build and maintain a website that provides a quick, effective and multi-device experience.

Digital success can often begin with your website and its ability to support user and search needs. This long-term tactic includes website maintenance, updates that coincide with technology innovations, and ever-changing user demands from a search and website experience and expectations. Items that you should consider as part of an initial and ongoing website performance-improvement strategy include website structure and architecture, content segmentation, main and supportive navigation, site speed, mobile friendliness, website coding and crawling and indexation efficiencies. The website may be a starting point for this; however, most websites will require initial and ongoing servicing as a minimum expectation of resource use, to encourage optimal value over the longer term.

Create data-driven, thought leadership content written for the users but with search engine optimization (SEO) in mind

When you create a functional and technically supportive website (as previously mentioned), the next step is making sure that users and search engines can understand the content. This step is imperative for accurate indexing, as well as creating potential for authority and ranking value to be derived from the content. A typical web page can be divided into a number of sections. The main ones are as follows:

- *Main content.* The main body content on the page, likely to be the driving topic and purpose of the page itself. Often combining a number of mixed content types, this is the main signal to users and search engines of the page's intent and the depth of value delivered.

- *Secondary content.* This can be varied in implementation, but as a general function, secondary or supplemental content supports the experience the page provides. This can include navigation functions, as well as content provision in areas such as expandable content (content that appears 'onclick' for example) and tabbed content, as well as other hidden content alternatives requiring action to view in full. Secondary content gives the users availability to access additional information surrounding (or supporting) the primary theme or topic. This often requires user exploration – ie scrolling the page, click-on navigation, or expanding 'onclick' content items.

- *Action content.* This type of content is nearly always supplemental to the main messaging of the page and can include items such adverts and goal-completion stages for the user to progress. As the name suggests, action content tends to focus on desired micro or macro user interactions and content engagement. As an example of this, an affiliate marketing website would have fairly dominant content that is advertorial action based.

- *Calls to action (CTA).* A call to action (or CTA) is a direct instruction to the website visitor to complete a next step. Calls to action can drive the user journey, improve click-through rates (ie the number of people completing actions (which will in most cases involve clicking at some stage)) and can help to extract value from the people who land on your web pages. An example of a call to action would be asking the user to 'click here for more information', or 'read the report now', or something less direct, for example 'find out more'.

At this stage it is useful to consider some of the factors needed to create content *that works* and I have included a few examples below. The tips and advice below are examples of action points, but do not restrict yourself to these – as there are many more possibilities:

- Make sure anything you add to your website is better that the best example you can find available – this may seem unattainable; however, this should be an aspiration.

- Depth of content matters. Complex industries, topics, products and services, require de-mystification and education. One to three thousand words are a good gauge of depth and value for core information pages – sometimes 'more' really is more.

- There are lots of search verticals available (news, blogs, video, maps and so on), and it is important to service them all. If you are only producing limited content types you *are* missing out.

- People digest content in different ways, so if you want your messaging to be truly accessible, you will need to provide alternative content access and digesting options.

- Content should be written for the user, delivered to people, and structured for search engine understanding and value application. Content can be effectively coded to support maximum search potential without any detriment to the user experience or enjoyment.

- If content has a genuine purpose, it should not be hidden. There are exceptions to this, but in most cases the point of content is to be found, read, shared and enjoyed. Content hidden for search gains will not form any likely long-term successful SEO tactic.

- All information for consumption needs to be accessible, regardless of the technology used to discover it, or of any languages, locations, knowledge levels and any physical impairments.

- Any information added to a website needs to be kept accurate, up to date and reflective of any industry change. Re-purposing content effectively is an important part of content and website maintenance.

- Content types can demand additional attention. For example, news content is expected to be relevant, frequent, timely and accurate. A blog post is expected to have an author, an opinion, and a reason for creation (all content should in fact have a reason for 'being'). Blog content should also be easy to share, comment on and interact with.

- All content needs to be unique, not copied or scraped from other sources.

- Quality is all important. Spelling, grammar, accuracy, expertise and many other signals support quality perception.

- Your content needs to answer questions, solve problems, educate audiences and encourage awareness and sharing.

Encourage user interaction, feedback, content generation; and facilitate social sharing/syndication

Content quality signals span a myriad of metrics. They include users spending long enough on the page to read the content, people viewing other pages on the site, interacting with the content, and very likely showing their satisfaction of the content by sharing and talking about it. A key stage for encouraging user actions is making an interaction and engagement as simple to complete as possible. Consider well-placed social sharing buttons and direct user guidance (including calls to action) to instruct the user on what you expect from them, rather than expecting them already to know.

Grow locally and expand; always maximize but never limit by location optimization

Most websites can make greater use of location as part of long-term strategy. Location is not restricted to physical addresses, but can be supported by them. Local growth can include your business networks and external interactions and be aspirational in addition to actual current location presence.

As a practical example of growing locally, consider Company C. Company C is based in a business unit in the south of the United Kingdom. It sells products online, as well as directly from its business premises. By aligning offline (actions not tied directly to their website or the internet in general) with online (their website in this instance) they can maximize location for driving expansion.

In this example, Company C adds a website address to its offline marketing (posters, brochures, business cards, stationery and so on), and this starts to encourage direct traffic and brand traffic to visit the website. The company adds to the website its full address, opening times and directions to its premises from important (known) selling regions and using different modes of transport (car, bus routes, trains and so on). This helps to drive new footfall to the business address, and encourages Google to understand that the business is relevant to certain location-based searches and search behaviour (eg people searching for that product on a mobile device near their location).

As the business grows, new location content is added to the site, as well as location-based supplier relationships, location-targeted customer reviews and online map listings. Location-specific directory sites also have the business included on them. Users and search engines can now see the added location value and relevancy to a number of search needs and the business can benefit online and offline from the tactics employed.

Think about what is not being said; putting persona and context in your search delivery

When you are highly sensitive to what your audience is seeking, and you provide the solutions to their needs, you start to become a required step in the search process, as opposed to an optional one. Once you begin to anticipate people's needs, fill holes in currently available information and start to create new conversations, you add longer term and ongoing opportunity as part of your digital strategy.

Every search vertical matters; serving them all effectively is not easy but can be effective

Each search vertical has a unique audience and offers an additional opportunity for your website, company, brand and service to expand its reach online. Users completing video search will have differing demands (and provide a new opportunities for gains) from those users digesting news, blogs or other content types. The more diversified you are in spanning search verticals, the more likely it is that you will be making better use of many of the broader aspects of the information seeking and buying process.

Linking on site and off site provides a network of signals that search engines cannot ignore

Like a vote in an election, links provide information about trust, popularity and authority. An external link from a relevant and trusted industry authority will pass value to the site it links to (assuming it is a 'followed' link). There are many link types and desired end results from links exceeding the basic attribution towards search ranking factors. An ultimate goal for a number of content-rich websites is the ability for content, and the website generally, to become naturally linkable. This objective of 'linkable content' requires many other content and quality characteristics to be satisfied (including many of those previously mentioned).

Short-term mentality

In contrast to longer term tactics, sustainable for repeated use and expected ongoing and long-term value on a majority of the resources used, the shorter term approach, seeks maximum initial value (or return). Often this reflects quicker impact tactics, even though a number of these tactics can also be repeatedly applied. The expectations from these shorter term tactics are closer to instant returns.

FIGURE 4.2 Short-term mentality tactics timeline (day one to day '90')

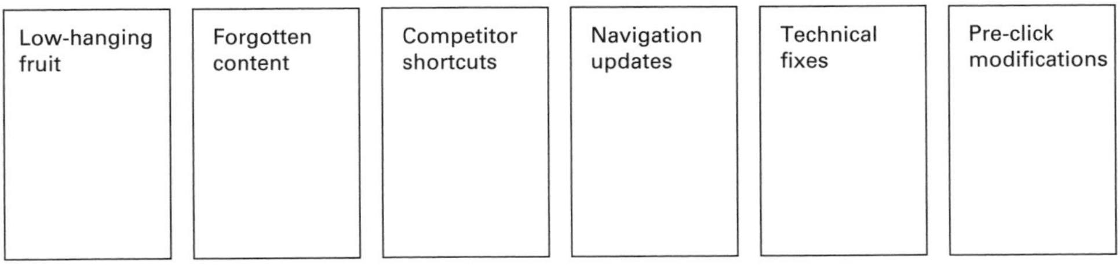

Low-hanging fruit	Forgotten content	Competitor shortcuts	Navigation updates	Technical fixes	Pre-click modifications

Grasping low-hanging fruit

Every business operating online misses out on some of the quickest wins from identifying and implementing actions based on easier (low-hanging) search opportunities. Every website I have worked on since 2003 has these instant win prospects and I strongly believe that there is no exception. Data, expertise, fresh perspective input and other strategy attributes help to get the most out of lower hanging fruit.

Finding forgotten content

When websites change over the years, content frequently gets buried, archived and orphaned off from the rest of the website. There are a number of ways to find orphaned content and to re-incorporate it in a website. Orphan content is simply content that is no longer accessible (or content that has been deleted from the live site) through any onsite links or navigation. For example, if your year-on-year (YoY) website traffic is down, it may be the case that previously contributing website content is no longer accessible. Bringing lost or forgotten content back to life is a fantastic way to add instant content contribution back into your website's performance.

Maximizing competitor short cuts

You do not need to *reinvent the wheel* every time you put together a search marketing strategy. One of the more personally and professionally challenging factors to consider is that sometimes a competitor *has* done something really well, and you can apply the logic and data from the competitor's approach to deliver success to your website. When it comes to search engine optimization, it can be a strength to recognize the contribution of others within your search environment, and to be able use this to help support your own future and ongoing successes.

Adding to the navigation

When you expand website navigation, you bring to the foreground content that was previously deemed less important, and introduce opportunities that did not previously exist. A static text navigation could reinvigorate layers of content on a website by incorporating some degree of dynamism. For example, adding drop-down navigation would provide depth of user and search value to parts of the site which would previously have required extra human and search effort to access them. There are many ways to build more into navigation, regardless of its current set-up.

Completing technical fixes

Technical fixes are never a one-off activity, but you can aim to implement a number of technical updates as part of a short-term strategy to improve search performance over a shorter time frame. Some of the first items to consider with technical website and search fixing include: broken pages and inaccessible areas of the website; slow pages and lack of mobile performance; barriers to crawling; thin and duplicate content, and much more.

Implementing pre-click modifications

When we speak about pre-click modifications, we are talking about ways to get your organic adverts to perform more effectively. A large element of this is title tag and meta description optimization, as well as items like rich snippet updates.

Every time your organic search adverts show up in Google and other search engines, you are presented with new data sets from which you can apply fresh logic, A/B testing and other actions for encouraging incremental and ongoing performance gains.

Many sites have missing meta data, duplicate information, brand heavy and repetitive meta data, plus other areas for improvement. Like most (if not all) short-term tactics, these are fully repeatable and necessary for long-term success. However, these types of updates have can have a beneficial impact that follows closely on initial implementation. This is one of the reasons why pre-click updates are included in most short-term SEO tactics.

Starting content promotion

Starting a strategic approach to pushing content out to wider, relevant audiences, and distributing your content more effectively, will support greater search success over the short term. If you already complete some form of content promotion you can always add new areas to your existing promotion and distribution channels, or improve your approach to content marketing and promotion.

When you are writing for people, ensuring those same people are able to read what you write about is paramount. From e-mail marketing and paid content promotion, through to social PR and RSS feeds, there are many tactics you can employ when embarking on content promotion.

Long term vs short term

The previous sections of this chapter have dealt with different tactics divided into long-term or short-term strategies. It is important to recognize that you can impact performance spanning day one to day 'n' ('n' meaning any number after one), and anywhere in-between.

The only choice posited so far has been the use of one (long term or short term) over the other, as opposed to a combination of both. In practice, however, it is important to recognize the independent value of each prior to considering the merits of using them both. The fact is that nearly all approaches to search engine optimization will be hybrids resulting in tactics that make use of both strategy timelines.

An SEO strategy is unlikely to be long term *or* short term (unless you have a fixed short time span to deliver on a very specific end result). Rather, the strategy is likely to combine long term *and* short term. Short-term wins can be important to establish customer trust and further investment, but excessive focus on the now, can lead to penalties and algorithm impact, restricting every other short-term opportunity until any impact has been resolved.

> A key SEO skill is to make the most of the now, while also being aware of the next step.

Creating a balanced SEO strategy – combining long-term and short-term tactics

There is never a single approach to creating effective SEO strategy. The approach taken needs to reflect a number of specific circumstances. These can include, but are not restricted to:

- what you are looking to achieve; your goals and objectives;
- the industry in which your business operates;
- the SEO industry – latest best practices and changes in opportunity;
- the latest data – this should always form part of your decision making;
- your unique value proposition;
- your current, potential and desired audience;
- the changing online competition.

When you apply a balanced search strategy to your approach to SEO, you are acknowledging both the strengths and the weaknesses of shorter and longer term tactics and integrating the two for greater potential search gains.

The following is a sample of a six-month balanced search engine optimization strategy. I have divided it into two quarters (Q1 and Q2), so that you can see how tactics can overlap, change and evolve as you gather new information.

The objective is neutral in this instance, as it is useful to see a varied number of tactics working towards a broader goal (search engine optimization). Applying this to your own search goals should be relatively straightforward as you become more familiar this technique.

Sample SEO strategy Q1

In the first three months an example SEO plan might be to:

- agree objectives, finalize business priorities and decide what a positive result would look like;
- ensure you are able to monitor, measure and report on key metrics;
- implement quick wins and maximize gains from lower hanging fruit;
- create a content editorial calendar for the first six months of SEO delivery;
- complete some pre-click updates to organic adverts;
- gather data to fuel decision making and strategy changes in Q2;
- benchmark, review and refine in preparation for Q2;

At this stage it can be useful to see an example of some of the above plan items (action points), so you can see how this turns into practical search implementation tactics.

Implement quick wins and maximize gains from lower hanging fruit

Regardless of how well established your website is, in what industry it operates, who the main competitors are, or any other scenarios tied specifically to your website, there will always be quick win opportunities in search engine optimization.

Some of the tactics associated with SEO quick wins, and lower hanging opportunities in general are discussed below. At this point it is necessary to understand that there can be hundreds of factors to consider in pursuit of shorter term SEO wins; so you should not limit or restrict your focus only to those suggested in this section.

The questions that you should be asking at this stage include:

- How long will this take to go live?
- What impact do I think this will have?
- In what order do actions need to be completed for maximum resource effectiveness?
- How much will this action impact total site performance.

Here are some example quick-win actions to consider as part of potential initial wins.

Finding and fixing broken content

Most likely this will be pages that are currently broken (404s) and either replacing that missing content with something fresh, relevant and value added, or redirecting that broken content to live pages on the current website.

Adding FAQs to current pages

This can be a quick and effective means to get fresh content and relevancy signals into existing landing pages, and a great chance to remove educational and conversion barriers from users' completed desired end results. Most websites offer some form of problem solving through their products and services and directly answering important audience questions can support a number of wins.

Adding internal links

This tactic can be used to prioritize content on your site, sending fresh value signals to the main search engines and logically tying related content together. Internal linking can be a quick implementation action. It can increase user engagement and content quality signals (eg increasing average page views per session), and can be a means to seed known user search queries relevantly into content.

Discovering and developing off-page mentions

Here we are looking at external websites that have mentioned your company (brand name, brand variation), website, or content you have created, but failed to link directly to it. While some brand value may be derived from mentions, most of the potential value is being missed. When you prioritize the sites to approach and successfully turn mentions into external links, you help increase search engine ranking factors from external votes of confidence as well as encouraging specific ranking gains (through areas such as link anchor text used), as well as referral traffic coming to the site.

Improve site crawling and indexation of content

This is a great thing to do for any website. Check how many pages are indexed (there are a number of ways to do this including 'site:' searches as well as checking data analysis tools like Google Search Console) and compare this to the total number of pages you have on your website. The difference between the two is an almost immediate win for getting new traffic to your site by fixing crawl and index issues.

Improving your organic adverts

In nearly every situation, the first three months of an SEO strategy will likely include SEO advert refinements and progression. Here we are talking primarily about title tag and meta description changes to support getting greater levels of clicks from impressions (traditional click-through rate optimization techniques).

On page optimization

There is a trend for content updates being associated with quick win tactics. This is perfectly logical, when you consider that one of the main delays (or time lags) between recommending website updates and positively impacting search engine performance is development time and backlogs. A feasible way to reduce this time lag is by applying a combination of initial tactics that include a weighting towards limited development time or technical needs. On top of this, content offers many positives towards many of the known and correlated ranking factors. On-page optimization can cover many updates, but in this situation, the focus is on header tags, above the fold content, important search term inclusion and adding mixed content types.

Benchmark, review and refine in preparation for Q2

These three steps are much more important than they appear at first glance.

Benchmark

Benchmarking from the outset helps provide clarity in terms of the current state of play. You need to know where you are now in order to project where you can feasibly get to within a six-month time frame. Benchmarks are imperative for assessing the next actions and for accurately assessing any improvements that have been made. It is important to have statistics for many more of the metrics than just those directly tied to your objectives and main key performance indicators. The reason for this is that implemented SEO actions may have a positive impact on wider success criteria than those initially anticipated and you should not overlook opportunity that can be repeated for the next phases of gains.

Review

Regular reviews need to be factored into any SEO delivery. You cannot evaluate progress made unless you have some degree of stock take as regards what you have done, what impact it had and how you can use this knowledge to achieve further advancement towards the overarching search goals. A review can take five minutes, or it may take half a day. This will vary depending on the scale of the project, the complexity of the objectives and the amount of input needed from all parties involved. If you are working collaboratively with a number of providers towards aligned objectives it is important that each of them contributes towards the review requirements. One of the main reasons for this is that everyone needs to have logical reflection points to consider the value that they are bringing to the project, the success of the actions completed and any alternative approaches and tactics required to fuel the next three months or more.

Refine

Refine, change, modify, reconsider, amend, adjust – there are many ways to interpret this point, and they all relate to making a change based on what you have benchmarked, what you have seen happen (reviewed) from the actions you have completed, and what you project will happen if you continue with the proposed next phase of the strategy. When you refine your SEO strategy you may be abandoning tactics that delivered limited, or no, tangible progress, or you may be increasing the focus on other tactics which over delivered compared to the time and resources invested in the first few months.

An understanding of ripples in search

Google introduced ripples to show the people/accounts who publicly shared content on Google+ and the people/accounts who re-shared that same content as *ripples* from the initial share. This feature was later removed in May 2015.

As a basic overview of the functionality of the Google+ ripple feature, accounts that have shared your content most frequently and to the largest audience, will appear as bigger circles (or ripples). Those sharing content less frequently, and with smaller audiences, will display as smaller circles (or ripples). If content did not have any shares and repeat shares, there was no ripple to view. There was also extra functionality which showed a ripple timeline to see how the shares/influencers and ripples changed over a given time frame.

You could access more data and interact with the influencer/sharer ripples to a greater extent than this. However, the information above provides an overview of the briefly available ripples feature from Google, so that you can see how it has been applied for a new and alternative theory and application in this book.

Search ripples

Search ripples are an extension of this previously available Google+ concept of visualizing the impact of one action (in this case an influencer sharing something) on an end result (ie the potential social reach of some form of content). It seems perfectly logical that you can apply this type of visual *ripple* application to other traceable interactions, including search engine optimization and this is what we will look at now.

Figure 4.3 provides an example of ripples in SEO – in this case ripples to show a number of actions impacting content quality.

When you consider the broader picture, and the hundreds of direct ranking factors for search engine optimization, plus the likely hundreds of correlating ranking contributors, you begin to understand the actual ripple effect in SEO.

I have chosen to use ripples as a visual device to help you think about the bigger search picture, and the interactions and impact of one action on another, all contributing towards an end result. One of the aims here is to make the theory more applicable to you and your requirements.

FIGURE 4.3 Search ripples: A sample of ripple types – content quality

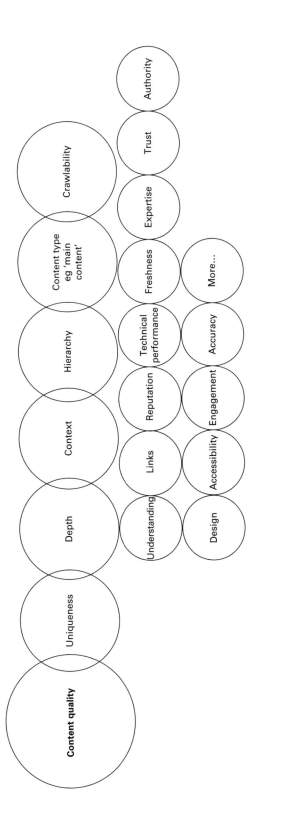

An important point to recognize at this stage is that action circles or ripples are sized to reflect the perceived potential impact (or if retrospectively applied, actual impact) on the end result. The bigger the action circle, the greater the likely impact on the end result.

For the sake of simplicity, the examples used show only a couple of size differentials. In a real approach and application, ripple sizes will be changeable in most cases.

Ripples reflect the current identified action areas and should be seen as a starting point from which to build in next phases of ripples (or actions). By creating ripples for search strategies, you can quickly identify threats, opportunities, weaknesses and strengths, as well as comparing the metric success of historical strategies to innovate and refine future ripple creation.

Practical examples of ripple creation

In the previous section, we introduced the concept of ripples in SEO, and more specifically in the area of ripples relating to content quality. In this section, you get to see some additional ripple examples spanning other important areas of SEO.

The main purpose of these additional examples is to reinforce the practical creation of ripples within search strategy, and to familiarize yourself with creating visual aids (in the form of ripple relationships) to take forward with your own approaches to SEO delivery.

You will notice that many of the ripple actions are transferable across end goals, and that smaller ripple actions for one goal type, may become larger ripple actions for another. When applying multiple ripples as part of a search strategy, you may find that prioritization of ripple actions needs to take account of the frequency and scale of these repeat ripples.

FIGURE 4.4 Search ripples: A sample of ripple types – website health

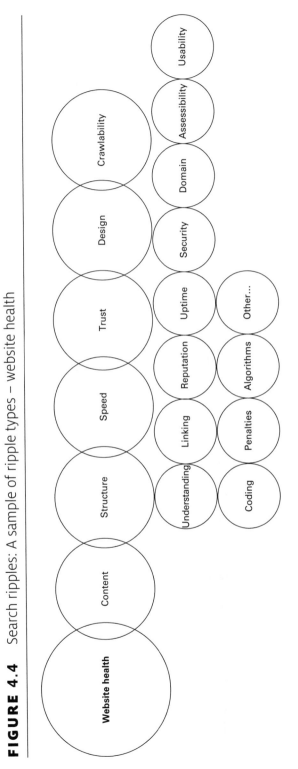

FIGURE 4.5 Search ripples: A sample of ripple types – local optimization (SEO)

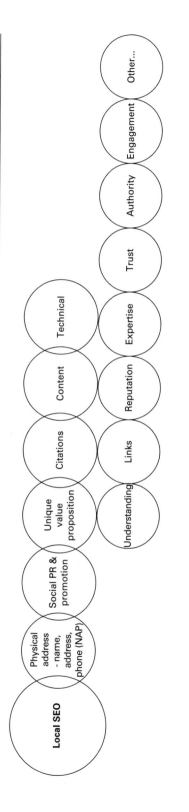

Key terms

Throughout this textbook you will be provided with brief explanations and bespoke definitions for some of the industry-specific terminology used. Some applications of terminology are unique to this book. For ease of reference, all of the definitions are listed in the order that they first appear in this chapter.

SEO delivery

This is the practical application of search engine optimization theory and strategy. SEO delivery may be specific to an individual, a company, any number of expert staff, resource providers and more.

Long-term search mentality

An intentional focus on the longer term approach for reviewing, delivering and looking at achieving search objectives. In many traditional SEO campaigns, the focus would have been weighted towards the longer term. One of the main reasons for this was the number of time lags potentially impacting the ability to demonstrate progression over the shorter term. Some examples of SEO time lags may include data collection, search engine re-crawling and re-evaluation of ranking gains, turnaround time for implementing SEO recommendations, and more.

Short-term search mentality

As you might expect, in direct contrast to longer term search mentality, this relates to quick, short-terms tactics that can support shorter time frame potential gains in search engine rankings. Every website will have some low-hanging fruit to use for faster results online. A good example of this could be redressing a number of broken pages (404s) to redirect authority to currently live pages and increase referral traffic coming to your website.

Ripple

The direct impact of one action on another, often referred to in relation to water and the series of water movements (or ripples) appearing after an initial impact or disturbance in the water. Dropping a pebble in a still pool will result in a number of ripples dispersing from the point of impact – a ripple effect.

Tactic

A specific action taken to impact a desired end result. Applying click-through rate optimization is a tactic used to generate more traffic from existing impressions.

Hybrid

The new end result of combining two distinct items. For example, combining a mixture of short-term and longer term tactics provides an approach to search strategy that is different to either in isolation.

Multi-device

People digest content using a number of technology types. While search has traditionally been limited to desktops, over the past few years a number of new technologies (specifically user devices) have enabled many (multiple/multi) forms of new search behaviours. People can search the internet on mobile phones, SmartPhones and tablets (for starters).

Search verticals

Search engines have individual means of segmenting content by types. You can view all types of content as part of a default web search, or you can refine your search to a search niche. Examples of search verticals include video, news, blogs and maps.

Thought leadership

A thought leader is someone or something (ie a business) who has a recognized value and authority within an area of expertise or opinion. Thought leadership content, is content that is created by someone/thing whose opinion/content is highly sought after and likely to be able to sway other less authoritative opinion on the subject matter.

Content promotion

The act of pushing, distributing and *promoting* something for broader reach, awareness and engagement. The ultimate goal from content promotion is some form of profitable (and ideally repeatable) end result.

Key points

- Digital success begins with your website and its ability to support user and search needs.

- Long-term vs short-term mentalities in search often lead to a hybrid strategy acknowledging the values of both.

- When you create a functional and technically supportive website (as previously mentioned), the next step is making sure that users and search engines can understand the content.

- Most websites can make greater use of location within long-term strategies.

- Each search vertical has a unique audience and offers an additional opportunity for your website, company, brand and service to expand its reach online.

- Like a vote in an election, links provide information about trust, popularity and authority.

- Every business operating online misses out on some of the quickest potential wins.

- You do not need to reinvent the wheel every time you put together a search marketing strategy.

- Search ripples are an extension of this previously available Google+ concept of visualizing the impact of one action on an end result. The bigger the perceived actions impact on the end result the greater the ripple.

- Ripples reflect the current identified action areas and should be seen as a starting point from which to build in next phases of ripples (or actions) – not an exhaustive or finite view of all the available actions.

Thinking about SEO in terms of value rather than ROI

LEARNING OUTCOMES

In this chapter we consider the role of SEO and specifically why it is important to make value the basis of an approach to search engine optimization, rather than return on investment (ROI).

After reading this chapter, you will have gained knowledge on:

- why value should always come first with SEO

- a by-product approach to delivering ROI from SEO

- sector-specific case studies, and how any website can add ROI from value in the low-cost marketing, travel and e-commerce markets

Why value always comes first

It can be a fairly common practice for SEO services to be completed almost exclusively, on the basis of a metrics-projected solution. For example 'I invest £x and get back £y'. In this type of situation '£x' can be single fee, a consultancy-based payment or monthly charges. You would then find that '£y' is usually a breakdown of measurements of desired outcomes such as traffic, goal completions, transactions and so on, *or* a percentage return on investment (ie for every pound invested, SEO returns one £1.20).

At first glance this approach seems to be perfectly logical. People investing in a service or expert resource want to know what they are expected to get back in return. One of the problems that can occur with a returns-based search engine optimization service (when you are primarily looking at SEO as an ROI vehicle) is the highly isolated and segmented actions-based approaches that get applied from SEO strategy. All too often, this then leads to a restricted level of service delivery.

The part of the SEO solution that needs to be present throughout, but is almost entirely overlooked in many ROI-driven approaches, is value.

> An excessive focus on the metric can constrain breadth of genuine value, undermine longer term success, and blinker expertise to the point of overlooking the obvious.

This may sound a little extreme; however, if your SEO is built on very specific metric returns, any deviation from actions directly impacting these metrics, is likely to be at a perceived loss (resource loss, time loss and ultimately perceived investment loss).

For example, if you have a leading metric of transaction increases, how will you be able to justify to a client the need to create blog content (just a single example of an action not tied to transaction-based ROI) that is traditionally a small (and sometimes zero direct) contributor towards transactions? In part, it is the constant justification of non-direct impact metric recommendations that will lead to the limitations of an ROI-based strategy.

Before we go any further, it is important to clarify that metrics *are* important in SEO focus, actions and delivery. Every SEO campaign should include goals, some form of agreed measurements of success (and improvement), and clarification of what success looks like to the customer – all of these areas will require metrics to be in place.

Metrics help to de-mystify what you are doing and why, as well as helping customers to understand some of the deliverables of what they are paying for, plus what they expect back from that payment.

What is more important, however, is how you work towards delivering on metrics and everything else surrounding the metric opportunities. While value is not the only omission in a metric ROI service approach, it is one of the most important areas, and therefore warrants specific attention.

Types of search metrics

As you might expect there are search metrics (or measurements) for almost everything online, so do not consider the following as the only options available to you. However, these cover some of the most common metrics used for SEO. At this stage it is useful to spend some time understanding metrics for SEO, as these will likely become one of the key reporting items and certainly a customer area for confirming or questioning success, regardless of your specific approach to delivery.

As you begin to progress through these metric types, please keep in mind that the metrics are the measurements of the results of the expertise, and the actions you apply within your search strategy; they are not the sole basis for generating results.

> Metrics are the measurements of the results of the expertise, and the actions you apply within your search strategy, they are not the sole basis for generating results.

Impressions

Directly attributable to SEO actions completed, impressions give you one of the earliest signals that the strategy you are working on is having some initial sign of positive impact.

Clicks

The desired immediate result of an impression is someone clicking on your advert and being (almost always) taken to a new destination outside of the SERPs. A click is the equivalent of footfall traffic in a traditional retail outlet.

SEO traffic

Also widely referred to as organic traffic. Not everyone clicking an item to land on your website will be coming from organic search (or SEO traffic). For example, searchers who have both paid (PPC) display options and organic display options will have a choice of which to click, leading to segmentation of types of traffic coming to your website. These are just two examples of traffic segmentation, but there are many more types, and some are discussed as other metrics of success in this section. The traffic entering your website from SEO as a distinct traffic type is very often a core, direct, measurement of SEO performance. Traffic can be measured in a number of ways including year-on-year (YoY) performance, which can assist with removing some of the potential external skewing factors like seasonality, as well as month on month (MoM), for fresher, and shorter period time frame comparisons.

Referral traffic

In most situations SEO focus and improvement will extend beyond the single traffic segment of 'SEO traffic'. Link building and additional off-page SEO-focused activity will directly impact the amount of traffic coming to the site from external websites. For example, you create some business entity links on far-reaching directory and citation sites (consider websites like Yell.com), all of the people that click on a website link from those websites will be allocated as *referral traffic*. Any content or information that you have linking to your website from an external resource will add to referral traffic volumes providing people enter the website directly from these external locations.

Direct traffic

As more people become aware of your brand (brand awareness is a key SEO deliverable), more people will in turn directly navigate to your website. When people type the website address directly into the browser address bar, or when return visitors use bookmarks and other means to return to your site, they will be allocated as *direct traffic*. Direct traffic can be an important trailing indicator for successful optimization of a brand online. Although direct traffic tends to be brand centric, it can also be a specific measurement of a service or solution improvement. For example, you promote a new service through an aligned content, social PR, e-mail marketing and optimization approach. You can track all of these specifically with changes to direct traffic (as well as referral, organic (or SEO traffic) and other traffic types).

SEO channel percentage of total website traffic

This becomes slightly more complex, as arguably, the more successful your SEO delivery becomes, the more positive its impact will be on direct and referral traffic (as well as other areas including traffic from social media). Having stated this, SEO contributing (as a specific traffic medium) towards greater percentages of the total (100 per cent) of website traffic is a regularly used measure of success. As an example of this, increasing visits from SEO as a channel from 30 per cent contribution to total site success, up to 55 per cent contribution, would see SEO in isolation, as the single, most important traffic-generating medium for the business. This type of statement is not possible without metric awareness in delivery.

Additional segmentation changes

There are many ways in which you can segment the traffic and users that visit your website; so identifying those that are more important to your organization and optimizing them, will result in campaign- and often customer-specific segmentation metrics. As a basic example of this, you may wish to optimize specifically for mobile-specific (or even device-specific) segments, and will need to report on the impact of this targeted optimization. Tactics within this approach would likely include mobile site speed, friendliness and responsive design.

Website well-being

SEO extends the basic role of a person seeing your advert, clicking on it, and buying something from you. Your website fulfils a key role in the ability to perform online, and the ability to facilitate a user experience. This experience must provide an end result(s), as well as many future, and directly related end results. From website speed, to broken links, and user experience, the *health* of your website provides many individual and collective means to benchmark, action and improve, tied to metrics.

Branded and non-branded

Whether you are looking at impressions, traffic, goal completions, transactions and so on, there is a need to differentiate between brand (ie company name, variations of company name, plus any key products and services with a brand of their own) and non-brand gains (everything excluding brand). A large brand is likely to experience growth within brand search engine optimization (often due to other marketing, PR and media activities, as well as general business growth) in addition to any directly attributable gains from SEO actions. However, when a small brand, new brand, or the same brand (as previously mentioned), launches into a new marketing niche, purchases a new subsidiary that does not fit with the brand, or moves into new territories, it loses a large proportion (potentially all) of its brand power, and needs to be able to adjust strategy to reflect a much more visible non-brand impact.

Micro and macro goal completions

Goal completions are any type of trackable end result. A macro goal completion is the final result; for example a form completion, a transaction or something final like a telephone call. Micro goal completions are any other type of action or interaction that can help progress someone towards a macro goal completion. An example of this could be a brochure download, watching a video, or reading terms and conditions required prior to a purchase. Adding an item to a basket can be seen as a micro goal completion, whereas finalizing payment would be the macro goal completion.

Consider the following practical example of micro and macro goals completions.

Company D drives 1,000 visits to a product page, but only 20 people buy that product. Following numerous tests, the business understands that there are key stages in the buying process which that page does not fulfil at present. Company D adds some micro goals to the page.

They add a video which has event tracking (a means to see how many people have engaged with that video – this can be added with Google Analytics as one free example implementation) to see how many people watch it prior to purchasing (the micro goal completion being visitors watching the video). They include a call to action to encourage people to watch the video (eg 'See how easy this product is to install').

Below the product there are some frequently asked questions (FAQs). To save screen space these are coded so that the user needs to click on them to see the answer. These FAQs cover the main barriers that people need to know to make a purchase without fear of making the wrong decision. Again, these have event tracking included in the code so that the business can see data on engagement in these micro goal completions (the micro goal being people reading the key FAQs).

Through testing the placement of these new micro goal completions and the content contained within them, Company D is able to refine its approach to converting on this page (in this example a conversion being a sale).

Why does value need to come first?

All of the previously discussed metrics can be directly impacted by building a strategy around value *first* and end results, or metric based ROI, *second*. A primary potential gain in doing so, is that value-based strategy evolves, changes and includes the whole audience.

Value-based strategy evolves, changes and includes the whole audience.

When trying to understanding value it is important to consider the many user influencers that are required to support end goals (in this context an end goal can be one of the earliest desired user actions including pre-click, ie a searcher clicking on an organic advert). In contrast to this, strategy focuses solely on the end metrics leads to very limited scope, variation or value derived.

A by-product approach to delivering ROI from SEO

There is a myriad of potential benefits in applying search engine optimization tactics to any website, and the vast majority of these benefits are not tied to ROI. However, SEO without ROI is not sustainable in most situations (looking at the longer term, or 'SEO over "n" time frame'). We focus next on delivery of ROI as a by-product of value-based search (or SEO) strategy.

> ROI is not a forgotten or hidden element of a by-product approach to a search strategy; in fact it is one that is considered in most tactics used. Moreover, metric ROI (in the form of a specific type of return from investment) as a by-product, shows the interdependent relationship that can exist between value and ROI.

> The following covers the range of influences and some of the types of actions (or tactics) that can be applied to service those influences in order to deliver ROI as a by-product of successful SEO. An influencer can be at any stage of the buying processes including before a user lands on your website or after a final purchase.
>
> Note that these are not placed in any specific order, as this will differ depending on the stage in the information seeking and buying process that the searcher is currently at, as well as a number of other external factors.

TABLE 5.1 SEO influences and actions supporting by-product ROI

Influencer	Action
Awareness of price, direct value comparison gains and a differentiator based on cost	Making prices clear, easy to locate and supported by any price-based value offering
Conveying trust, credibility and satisfaction of financial safety needs	Providing secure payment, a secure website and clearly satisfying user trust needs
Ability to find out more, research alternatives and reinforce the initial intent to act (click/purchase/download etc)	Delivery of depth of content. Intuitive and hierarchical navigation, as well as clearly topical segmented information
First impressions: look, feel, authority and other stimulators	Professional design, unique imagery, active white space and inclusion of known audience information needs
Risk. Level of total cost incurred to the user. This can include time/resource cost as well as financial and more	Defining expected time to an expected end result and breaking down actions for easy completion. Reinforcing of trust through content, case studies and more
Satisfaction of personal safety needs. Tied in part to financial safety but more encompassing, this will include data security and the ability to act without unwanted next actions	Supplemental information elements to remove trust barriers to success. Often in the footer or sub-menus, items may include terms and conditions, company value, data protection and more
A broader knowledge of other people's actions in the same scenario, who went on to convert and the benefits or satisfaction derived – the impact of herd mentality	Providing user-generated content. Reviews, cases studies, social PR
Customer help, support and problem resolution – availability, access and completeness	The availability of clearly defined support including telephone, e-mail, live chat, physical address

TABLE 5.1   *Continued*

Influencer	Action
Incentives. Tipping-point justifiers. Often including something for free, this can help overcome any outstanding barriers to action	Free postage, multi-purchase offers (buy one get one free/BOGOF), limited time discounts, seasonal sales
Quality perception. This can be an isolated assessment or comparative to available alternatives	Star ratings, independent reviews, user videos, product testing, research and analysis
Social signals. In part this will include herd mentality, but it also includes access to broader peer information, feedback and encouragement to act	Providing easy information sharing and syndication. On-site product and service feedback as well as other social signals like comment functionality
Longer term relations. This can include the desire to return, repeat interact and become a valued consumer	Repeat purchasing encouragement, ongoing communication after end result and drip feeding contact
Quick and easy information access and digestion, reflecting the unique user preferences	Supplying mixed content types for multi-device and content rich experiences – often the more exhaustive the better
Efficient, understandable journey – the ability to complete an end result without additional thought processing	Clear calls to action, micro and macro goal completions, a logical and efficient consumer check-out process
Customization, alternatives and the opportunity to include personalization or variation to the situation	Give the user the chance to have a more tailored and personal experience; this can include user engagement and selection criteria as well as filter options for products, content and other areas
Upgrades, improvements, modifications and extras. Something better, new or differentiated to alternatives	In many cases this will be final selection changes, upsells, and other areas. This can also include the awareness of new products, ranges and the latest product or service improvement areas

Sector-specific case studies – ROI from value

Since graduating in Business Management and Communications back in 2003, I've had the opportunity to deliver search marketing and wider digital solutions, in-house, as a start-up business, working as a consultant, and heading up a search (SEO specialist) department for a leading UK search and digital agency.

In this time, I have trained search and marketing specialists, outsourced digital services, run and fulfilled a key part of hundreds of multi-disciplinary expert search and digital marketing campaigns, and worked on search solutions for websites spanning every industry I can think of.

The purpose of this section of the book is to share some of the search-sector tactics that have worked in these industries, which are also applicable for other search niches. The focus in this part of the chapter is to provide you with a *normalized* strategy example covering some of the most competitive industry types. In this case, low-cost marketing and the travel industry, as well as a website sector type (in this example e-commerce websites).

The strategy examples provided are not specific to any single business in which I have been involved for the purpose of delivering search marketing success. These case studies are based completely on a hybrid of tactics that I have experienced in delivering success specific to these and other industries over a number of years. In addition to this, tactics in these instances may include suggested and potential opportunities, as well as any retrospective opportunities based on implementation.

At this stage, it is important to understand that the following are not complete strategies. They are tactics that can enhance your success in these and other online marketing segments. All of these tactics have value opportunity extending the practical example for which they have been used in this context, and in fact, the more creative you become with adapting online tactics like these, the greater the potential value you will have over many years when deploying and refining them.

My intention is to help you identify bespoke tactics for search engine optimization, to refine them, and understand how these tactics can be applied and adapted for your requirements.

CASE STUDY   Low-cost marketing industry

The low-cost marketing niche is a highly competitive industry online. Although this tends to focus on e-mail marketing, there are a number of additional low-cost marketing segments within this broader topic, and I consider them all in the strategy overview detailed below.

Comparison

When you are competing in a highly competitive industry, and offerings can appear to the searcher to be identical (apart from messaging), differentiation can become a core search opportunity. The greater the depth of comparison and statistical/factual base of the comparison, the greater the potential gains can be. Variation of the means of delivery and content type for comparison can be used for multiple tiers of success. For example, lists and tables can give easy access to quick comparison features, details and top-level information, but the use of screen recordings and user videos can add depth of content types as well as alternative means to provide information on more complex features that may require some degree of familiarity and knowledge on the topic.

Seasonality

Building a degree of seasonality into the main site hierarchy can support the capture of opportunity beyond the industry alone. Low-cost marketing is driven by the need to communicate, and what better way to broaden reach and awareness than through repeat calendar events? Easter, Christmas, Thanksgiving and other mainstream events are great starting points; however, the tactic becomes even more effective when incorporating less obvious ones. Think about opportunities such as business sector trends and events, consumer peak buying periods and more.

Integration

With the alignment of marketing channels (in this case e-mail/other low-cost marketing types and SEO) you can support marketing communication with website information, education and offerings, far exceeding the opportunity within an e-mail/mailshot/other in isolation. When you introduce a multi-disciplinary approach to communication, you are able to counteract the limitations of one medium with the benefits of another. This type of approach can be especially useful for longer conversion journeys, where you need to drip feed interest over longer time frames; but it can also be effective when looking to drive immediacy of action.

Segmentation

Often, when working in an *all-sector-inclusive* scenario like low-cost marketing, one of the biggest challenges can come from trying to cater for every opportunity in every location. Core, top-level pages, including the home page can be some of the more daunting prospects for effective segmentation; but when you get this right, the continuous expansion of segmented sector/user/persona opportunity becomes a strategy foundation. Effective segmentation can involve many forms of implementation including bespoke or dynamic content delivery, main and sub-navigation, sub-folder and even sub-domain segmentation (added to all of this can be design, content, and other forms of user guiding strategy).

Data

When you are creating unique audience value, one of the most successful resources can be your own data collection, analysis and research/reporting. Low-cost marketing companies often have some of the deepest volumes of information available ready for analysis and reporting to the market. When this data is maximized it can give true insight, opinion and company voice, providing a clear educational and thought-leadership advantage over the competition.

CASE STUDY   Travel industry

One of the most challenging industries in which to succeed online is the travel sector. This is due to the volume and variety of competition, combined with some of the largest and most recognizable competitors in the marketplace. The tactics discussed below include some opportunities to add distinct search and user value within this niche. These tactics, like all the others provided in this chapter, are also applicable to other situations and sectors. They have been proposed based on the potential application for gains more pertinent to these sectors.

Streamlining

In this sense we are looking at ways in which user information can be hollowed out into practical packages, unique to user needs, with the maximum amount of relevancy, and the minimum amount of user effort needed to digest the information. Travel consumers will likely require a lot of shallow-level help and advice and will buy in packages, so providing information in the same manner, supports efficient search and buyer behaviour. An example of this is the packaging of transport, accommodation, consumables and insurance as a single packaged holiday option. This often combines third-party services into a single customer-facing service – the same can be achieved with content, user journey, conversion paths and more.

Price

Travel niches can be notoriously sensitive when it comes to price. The driving forces behind this are the widespread access to product comparison sites, and the relatively short time frames from which decisions to purchase are often made. From flights and hotels, to insurance and car hire, successful price positioning is imperative. It is important to understand that positioning of price is not the same as needing to provide the cheapest price. Price can be used as effectively as a sign of quality and service, as it can be as a low-cost immediacy signal for action. When looking at price-based tactics for SEO, think about transparency of pricing, supporting content and justification of pricing and secondary tactics to reduce or increase pricing options throughout the buying process.

People

Stories sell when it comes to the travel industry, and the best way to tell a story is through real people. You may be fortunate (or have worked very hard) to have existing and naturally increasing brand advocates, but for many this gap in advocacy can become an unseen barrier that limits search success in this sector. There are many tactics that can be employed to create new brand advocates and discover hidden advocates. Some of the more successful opportunities can include providing free products and services to leading bloggers and target personas for reviews and social PR, running competitions, providing content sharing and brand engagement incentives and more. With travel, the more you can look to tie the tactic to something creative, the better the outcome will often be.

Verticals

Here we are looking at making use of the more creative search verticals such as image search and video search. People's early information seeking can start with a stunning visual; anything from a smiling face to a desolate landscape. Imagery in all its manifestations comes to the fore within the travel sector. Images and video are not only for destination searches, however; think about the impact of short video reviews, and image-based competitions for persuading a website visitor to sign up for that last-minute holiday.

Newsjacking

In the context of this tactic, 'newsjacking' refers to the ability to take very current and newsworthy events to leverage your reach, engagement and website traffic opportunity, by turning around quick (most likely on-site) content, to service short-term peaks in new user search volumes. This can be traditional media outlet news, television trends, and realistically, any type of new, and short-term, event that triggers new volumes of search interest. When you are able to create unique, on-trend content, fast and effectively, as well as merging a unique stance, expertise and opinion, with a variety of trending mainstream topics, you will be likely start to have the potential to rank highly across many, diverse, but still relevant travel themes.

CASE STUDY   The e-commerce sector

In this context, e-commerce websites are simply sites that sell directly to the consumer through the website that the searcher landed on directly from the search engine results pages. Such websites are known for huge volumes of very shallow content, and the focus on the end of funnel audience segmentation. E-commerce websites rank highly through the thousands (potentially millions) of search queries specific to product ranges, and the challenges facing them can be substantial.

Categorization

When you have a large site spanning thousands (or millions) of product ranges, one of the most important tactics to get right from the outset, is the top-level creation and segmentation of product ranges. The goal at this stage is to have a set of targeted category pages of the website that logically group content/products together for easy user filtering and clear search theming.

Product differentiation

An important part of getting a breadth of products to rank online is to provide product-level information value that is greater than any of the competition. This seems like an impossible task when you have thousands of unique products to consider, but it can be achievable, even over the shorter term. Many content management systems (CMS) and database coding items will enable rules-based information to be included on desired pages site wide. The prerequisite is to identify the unique data that will add value, and ensure that it is effectively implemented for search and user gains. Product descriptions are some of the key focus areas in this tactic; however, there are also more chances to build in both rules based, and manual product updates outside of this remit successfully.

Prioritization

Regardless of the size of the website, some product ranges will contribute more towards ROI and total website success than others. When you have a finite amount of resources available, you need to ensure that the actions you take, and the pages/sections on which you focus, deserve that attention before other alternatives, and that the resource investment reflects the potential outcomes achieved.

Entire funnel focus

Many e-commerce sites focus on the bottom-of-funnel opportunity in isolation and this is a mistake. While bottom-of-funnel search focus will deliver the quickest and most immediate returns on investment, the remainder of the funnel will most likely deliver greater volumes of transactions and cheaper (time/resource/money) ongoing wins. By adding to the site content that supports the range of information seeking and buying needs, you expand the potential reach and visibility for the website, the brand, and many of the associated product ranges being sold.

Image optimization

If you are successful in image optimization at template level within your e-commerce website, you may be able to gain more visibility from images than any other content type on the site. Images need to be high quality, unique to you (rather than stock photos or standard stockist images), website ready (compressed, correct file types and more) and easy to share, engage with and purchase from. Every image should serve a purpose, tell a product story and support visual information in order to encourage immediate buying. Images should be accurately described in alt text, surrounding content and any supportive details provided.

Social sharing

The role of social media and social sharing is often overlooked as a search tactic for e-commerce digital marketing. Images are a useful driver for content sharing, syndication and engagement but, you should not restrict yourself to image social reach alone. There are a number of other shareable content types, and they all have distinct benefits. Video is rarely used to its optimum potential outside of clothing/fashion/design led e-commerce websites, but it can be one of the quickest tactics to deploy at category and key product level.

Key terms

Every chapter in this book contains industry jargon as well as concepts and terms that may not be familiar to you in the context of search engine optimization. For ease of reference, all of the definitions are listed in the order that they first appear in this chapter.

By-product approach (to ROI)

In the context of this chapter, a by-product approach to ROI reflects a secondary focus on ROI, while the main focus is on other areas of delivery. In this chapter, the primary focus of the approach to SEO is value.

Metrics-projected solution

This refers to the delivery of an SEO solution based primarily on estimated (or projected) potential gains. The measurements (or metrics) decided upon and estimated at the outset of the project outset may differ depending on the goals and desired outcomes from the search investment. Likely metrics would include ranking gains, traffic and conversions (sales or other goal completion type).

Low-cost marketing

This relates to alternative forms of marketing where the level of investment is minimal, or often free. Some of the more frequent types of low-cost marketing solutions include e-mail marketing and mobile phone marketing (text/SMS marketing).

e-Commerce

e-Commerce simply means electronic commercial transactions – in this case specific to monetary transfers completed on the internet. E-Commerce facilitates the successful transferring of funds for the buying and selling of goods and services online.

Micro and macro goal completions

Goal completions are any type of trackable end result. A macro goal completion is the final result, for example a form completion, a transaction or something final like a telephone call. Micro goal completions are any other type of action or interaction which can help progress someone towards a macro goal completion. An example of this could be a brochure download, watching a video, or reading terms and conditions required prior to a purchase. Adding an item to a basket can be seen as a micro goal completion, whereas finalizing payment would be the macro goal completion.

Metric (search metric)

A metric is a specific measurement which enables you to attribute gains or losses. For example; you add new content to a page on your website and after that change traffic (as a metric) increases. There are many search metrics which have common uses in identifying a search marketing campaign as a success or failure, and a number of these have been covered in this chapter.

Impression

Every time a user sees a search engine results page (SERP) on which your advert is displayed, this will count as an impression. For example, a searcher is looking at page two of a search engine results page for the query 'plumber London', and your organic advert appears in 16th place. This triggers an impression (or advert view). An impression is different from a click, as there is a difference between a searcher *seeing* your advert and *clicking* or engaging with it.

Multi-disciplinary

A combination of various and usually separate and distinct fields of expertise, for example aligning SEO and e-mail marketing. This can involve several disciplines; however, the important aspect is that each discipline is included for the potential complementary advantage that it brings to the situation.

Seasonality

A repeated (yearly) occurrence, usually a form of an event that can be predicted for future impact (positive or negative). For example, every year in February (Valentine's Day and the preceding few days) the retail sector will experience an increase in sales for seasonal cards, flowers and chocolates. By having access to data for correlating this seasonality, you can prepare for, often impact, and potentially improve on, the value derived from the seasonal opportunity.

Persona

The interpretation of the elements that make up a person's characteristics. In search marketing personas are frequently used in order effectively to identify, target and create strategy, to positively impact with products, services and solutions. A single product can be pitched to any number of different personas, but typically, a website will target very clear top-level personas and these will directly impact tone, style, creative and other messaging areas.

Newsjacking

The ability to bring new reach, engagement and visibility to your search strategy by being repeatedly seen in line with a diverse number of news-related topics. This is generally the shorter term ranking on very topical trends to support brand, site and service potential gains. While traffic gained from newsjacking can bring with it relatively high bounce rates and limited initial engagement, wider value can often be seen for general correlation with volumes of ranking success and other visibility-based metrics.

Key points

- Too frequently, SEO services are provided on the basis of a metrics-projected solution.

- The problem with returns-based service delivery in SEO (or only considering SEO as an ROI vehicle) is the highly isolated and segmented actions-based approaches that get applied.

- The excessive focus on the metric, constrains breadth of genuine value, undermines longer term success, and blinkers expertise.

- Every SEO campaign should include goals, agreed measurements of success (and improvement) and clarification of what success looks like to the customer.

- Metrics are the measurements of the results of the expertise and the actions you apply within your search strategy; they are not the basis for generating results.

- There is a myriad of potential benefits of applying search engine optimization tactics to any website, and the vast majority of these benefits are not tied to return on investment.

- It is possible to create strategies and tactics that are particular to an online niche or industry sector. Over many years creating search strategy, it becomes clear that some tactics are especially effective in particular industries.

- Re-purposing tactics and getting creative with strategy implementation can provide ongoing wins over many years, regardless of your business niche.

Creating a value checklist for SEO 06

LEARNING OUTCOMES

Once you have completed this chapter you will have a more thorough understanding of:

- what an SEO value checklist is
- how to create your own value-based checklist
- using the value matrix.

What is a value checklist?

So far we have covered what SEO is and why it matters; and we have talked about the benefits of achieving results online. We have looked into the deeper guiding principles of Google, the often interdependent relationship between SEO and Google, and provided a checklist for optimizing with Google in mind.

We have also examined the limitations resulting from excessive process within SEO delivery. We have looked at an alternative approach to implementing organic search marketing, and looked at techniques for identifying, amplifying and implementing additionalsearch opportunity.

You have been introduced to a new and evolved theory of 'search ripples'; we debated a long-term vs short-term mentality for SEO, and supplied some practical examples of ripple creation. One aim of this was empowering you to take this theory forward, and apply this in your own search engine optimization tactics.

In Chapter 5, we discussed a few of the reasons why value always comes first for long-term search engine success. We provided clarity on how to create a by-product approach to delivering ROI from SEO. You also had access to several sector-specific case studies, so that you could start to identify tactical opportunity for repeated search gains.

While 'value' has been a consistent point of reference throughout many of the previous topics covered, we haven't given you a practical guide for applying value comprehensively, as part your search approach – but that is about to change.

There are a million and one ways to create a checklist, to collate and group actions, and to provide experience-based logic to justify the purpose and inclusion (ie the merit) of each one. From experience, there are four key items that create a value-based checklist for search engine marketing: website value, user value, search engine value and business value.

When you cover these four core matrix elements, you can be confident that your value strategy has enough focus and diversity to deliver the required outcome.

FIGURE 6.1   SEO value matrix

Website value	User value
• Technical health and maintenance • Site speed • Architecture/navigation • Security/trust • Availability • Design	• Accessibility • Content • Audience/persona • Proposition • Communication • Journey • People needs fulfilment
Search engine value	*Business value*
• On page • Off page • Search verticals • Mobile	• Objectives/aims/benchmarks • Data/refinement/improvement • Location/brand/service/product • Returns (metrics/ROI)

Your step-by step-creation guide

The remainder of this section provides a checklist that you can use as the primary guide for ensuring that key tactics are not overlooked. As with all checklists, this example is not an exhaustive list of every factor that can positively impact your search engine optimization delivery. However, this can be used as an initial template for value strategy creation, or as a starting point for applying your own creativity towards objective attainment through SEO.

We start by looking at expanding on the website value matrix, and turning this into your first value checklist.

FIGURE 6.2 Website value checklist

Technical health and maintenance	**Security/trust**
Browser compatibility	Cookie policy
Tracking in place for data intelligence	Terms and conditions
Code error free/efficient/up to date	Data protection
Meta data present, unique, optimized	Privacy policy
Broken pages	Physical address
Broken images	Registered company
Broken content	Secure from hacking
Broken links (on site/off site)	Plugins up to date
Orphan (inaccessible) pages	Correct permissions
Content/URL duplication/canonicalization/	Appropriately hosted
cannibalization/	
Follow/nofollow linking	
Redirects/functional/purpose/	
implementation	
Maintain: speed/crawling/navigation/	
security/availability/design	
Page structure	
Clean/friendly/concise URLs	
Keywords: discovery/density/variation/	
synonyms/opportunity/context/relevancy	
Links (internal/external)	
Algorithm/penalty/best practices	
Broken page/URL/content handling/custom	
404	

Site speed	**Availability**
Desktop speed	Site uptime
Mobile speed	Crawling
Server level	Indexation
Site level	Accessibility – users/bots
Page level	Content inclusion/exclusion
Entity level	

Architecture/navigation	**Design**
Readable/text alternative provided/required?	Responsive
Logical order/priority/intuitive/common	Best practices
sense	Readable
All content access	Accessible
Minimized clicks/user actions required to	Optimized
end result	User friendly/driven
Logical location	Purposeful/reason
User driven/friendly	Distinctive/impactful
Inclusive	Brand specific
Clear functionality/expectations (on hover,	Persona driven
on click etc)	Supporting user journey/experience
Brevity of information	Engaging/mixed content types/social/
Data and user driven	shareable/linkable
Optimized/over-optimized – for the user/for	Use expectations/end results expected
search engines (both?)	
Clear topics/themes/inclusion criteria	

Next, it is time to consider the user value matrix.

FIGURE 6.3   User value checklist

Accessibility	Communication

W3C compliance
Cross-browser and device compatible
Print/offline friendly
Text alternatives for flash/video/
    JavaScript content
Content descriptive coding (including alt text)
Adjustable (fonts/styles)
Screen reader compatible
HTML site map available
Web ready (colours/styles/more)
Content compressed (downloadable
    regardless of connection speed)
Optimized/crawlable/indexable/structured
	Easily shareable/really simple syndication
	    (RSS)/social media ready
	Engaging/encouraging interaction
	Clear takeaways
	Skim readable
	Promoted/easy to discover
	Creating a story/selling the origination
	    intent

Content	**Journey**

First impressions
Most important content clarity and hierarchy
Digestible in varied forms
The best example available/thought and
    industry leading
Fresh/current/topical/seasonal
Accurate/relevant/supported by fact
Credible, thoughtful and well researched
Unique
Use of statistics
Long form/depth of value
Variation (of content types and reflecting
    user stages of information and buying
    funnel)
Available (as opposed to hidden, broken, or
    otherwise unavailable)
Planned in advance/scheduled/repeatable/
    recurring and expectable (time frames
    and more)
Design/styles/consistencies/predictability
	Able to access within relevant areas of the
	    website (site structure elements as well
	    as other natural internal linking)
	Hubs of self-contained information
	Minimal extra user actions required
	User guidance/instructions
	Help/support/problem solving
	Encouraging next actions, other content
	    digestion, furthering the journey

Audience/persona	**People needs fulfilment**

All inclusive (removal of familiarity/
    education barriers and jargon)
Identifiable by the intended users
Segmented to targets
Real language variation/context/regionalism
Safe for all audiences (or protected
    accordingly)
Location targeted/translated/global
Reflecting searcher/industry/topic trends
Entertaining/appealing
	Primary and secondary content levels present
	Access to external topic content
	Authorship/real people/expertise/brand
	Facilitating comments/feedback/
	User-generated value/surveys/forms
	Revisited/refined/improved/updated
	Providing a reason to return
	Page/content usability: testing, refining,
	    improving
	Messaging testing (A/B, split, multi-variant,
	    other)

Proposition	
Created for audience/persona (tone/style/ pitch) Driven by purpose/goals/objective/reason Provision of something meaningful	

At this point we consider some traditional checklist items for search engine optimization. With over 200 items considered in the Google ranking algorithm alone (direct/causation factors), ignoring all of the correlated signals and other areas, these checklist items provide a solid overview of some of the core consideration elements directly tied to search engine value.

The interpretation of 'on page' SEO in the example checklist below has been anything directly tied to the page in question.

FIGURE 6.4   Search engine value checklist

On page	Off page
Meta data/title tags	Business/service/brand/entity signals
Headings/structure	Mentions/citations/co-citations
Image alt text/naming conventions/ compression/uniqueness/enhancement	Reviews/trust/user
	Backlinks:
Website-ready content/coding/design and sparing use of Flash and associated items	existing, new, potential
	direct linking, functional, optimized
Content (depth/value/uniqueness/authority/ opinion/expertise/variation/types/story/ more)	best practice/algorithms/penalties, varied, relevant
	natural, social, PR
Mixed media/mediums/information digesting	anchor text, surrounding content, other
Crawling/discovery/indexing	Monitoring/tracking/engagement
Accessibility/compliance	Social media/PR/promotion
Functionality/operability/understanding	Reputation management/PR/other
Primary/secondary/surrounding/user-generated content	Location/community/conversation
	Technical discovery/fixing/enriching (links/ mentions/citations/more)
Context/synonyms/variation/expectations/more	Events, trends, seasonal
Identifiable and recognizable information types (navigation, links, styling, more)	Multi-channel integration
Depth/value/purpose/reason	
Header status accuracy, custom 404, error handling and associated items	
Permalink set-up/structure/topic/keywords/ variation/relevance/expectations	
User/audience/persona focus and optimization	
Speed/performance	
Design/usability/logic	
Technical health and maintenance	
Architecture and navigation	
Security, legitimacy, address, contact options and trust	
Schema/rich snippets	
Linking/positioning/interaction	
Content and linking best practice/algorithms/ penalties	
Topics/keywords/theme	
Data collation, tracking and intelligence	
Quality and improvement; surveys, forms, feedback	
User help/assistance/question answering/ barrier removal/support	

FIGURE 6.4   *Continued*

Search verticals	Mobile
News	Friendly/usable/compatible
Blogs	Optimized
Maps	Journey
Images	Speed/performance
Video	Content delivery and organization
Integrated (ie knowledge graph, answers, social, other)	
Multi-channel and integration/amplification	

Finally, we review business value. This tends to be less frequently discussed, but has a clear requirement within the value-based matrix.

FIGURE 6.5   Business value checklist

Objectives/aims/benchmarks	Location/brand/service/product
Purpose of the page/site/content/optimization/ actions	Establishing a unique business proposition
Positioning within the online niche/digital space	Maximizing for (not restricting by) location/ physicality
Intention of strategy and tactics deployed	Setting a tone, messaging, house style and recognizable voice
Clarity on expected results and measurements of determining success	Promoting your location/brand/service/product messaging
Analysis of the current state of play	Adding something new to the niche
Realistic and aspirational end results	Supporting/sharing business values and culture
Micro and macro goal identification/tracking/ improvement	Delivering consistent branding (logos, styles, design, more)
Performance of the website as an entity	Comparison, review, differentiation
Page, section, site performance	Full information and buying funnel reach, awareness and targeting
Required, desired, ego needs	Social monitoring, reach, engagement and impacting
Gains provided to the industry/audience	PR/brand/reputation monitoring, reach, engagement and impacting
Aligning and maximizing marketing channels	Legality
Building trust, authority and followership	
24/7 universal business access	
Educating, clarifying, de-mystifying and removing knowledge barriers	
Search engine, user, website, business value	

Data/refinement/improvement	Returns (metrics based/ROI)
Setting up data collection	While these will always be tied (at least in part) to objectives, goals, aims and benchmarks, there are a number of consistent metrics that appear within SEO and a few of these are detailed below.
Putting in place processes for data integrity and refinement	
Establishing effective ways of mining data for making decisions and taking action	
Setting up reporting from data tied to objectives, aims and benchmarks (primarily)	Impressions (all relevant search types)
Using the above to encourage and support improvement	Traffic (many/all relevant segments)
Monitoring, benchmarking, projecting, improving	Micro goal completions (anything contributing to page value)
Generation; surveys, questionnaires, feedback	Macro goals completions
On-site search (popularity, trends, gaps and opportunities)	Brand/non-brand
Handling, storing, trust, protection and security	Online/offline
	Performance improvements (website/search/ perceived/actual/user/business/more)
	Competition (comparative gains)
	Opportunity attainment (realization of potential)
	E-commerce end results (traditional sales wins)
	Repeat actions and future gains (repeat/return metrics)
	Meaningful data collation
	User-generated content
	Reach, awareness, sharing and syndication
	Sign-ups (newsletters, guides, e-mail lists, more)
	Site quality improvements

Questions to ask

Usually at this closing stage of a chapter we would provide key terms used within the section, however, the simplified checklists are based in large part on terms and tactics already covered in earlier parts of the book.

What may be of more use to you is a list of the types of questions that you need to be asking yourself when you are applying some form of checklist element to your delivering of an SEO solution.

One of the reasons for this approach is that the checklists themselves need to be regularly reviewed, refined and adapted, and this only becomes possible when you have a predictable level of questioning in place.

Here are a few questions to get you going ...

Why are you completing this action?

If the only reason you are adding a tactic/action to your strategy is that it is included on your checklist, you need to question the reason for its inclusion. If you have a team of people adding to a checklist, or when you create checklists by committee, it is likely that some checklist items have been *settled for* and on limited resources or time/budget availability; you will want to make sure every action counts and contributes.

What was the impact of this action last time?

An important part of strategy delivery lies in having an understanding of what happens and why. When you implement tactics you need to record, report and review them. An important part of any checklist delivery area, is the ability to prioritize actions, and include an aspect of repeatability (and predictability) of expected outcome.

What's next?

There should never be an end to SEO. Optimization means making something better. You should always be asking yourself 'what can I do next time?' You should not limit your approach by finishing your service with the end of a checklist. Remember that these checklists are the starting point for delivering a value-based approach to search engine optimization; they are by no means an all-encompassing guide to completing (or getting to an end point in) SEO.

What are you looking to achieve? And why?

These are some of the most pertinent questions you need to ask yourself. If you can only think of metric-based ROI areas when answering this question, you need to consider a more holistic view of optimization.

What did you achieve?

Ask yourself this question for the business, the audience, the industry, the niche and broader basic needs.

What does search utopia look like?

And how far away from it are you? Having an idealistic vision of what the perfect search scenario looks like, helps you to think outside of the box, and to think big. If traffic and transactions have increased by 50 per cent, what could have been done better to take this to 100 per cent? Is 100 per cent improvement enough? What would the total/perfect opportunity look like?

What did your audience (visitors/users/conversations/feedback/more) think?

Did you meet or exceed expectations? How positive are the interactions and feedback you are receiving? How often are people coming back for more? How naturally shareable, linkable and engaging are you becoming?

Key terms

SEO value checklist

A methodical template approach to delivering an SEO strategy based on value as the primary purpose. A checklist enables a process-driven approach to completing the same set of fundamental actions to encourage repeated (or expected results). Checklists are great for action reminders, and specific areas to be considered as part of your SEO value project.

Matrix (value)

The way a value matrix has been used in this section of the book is to demonstrate a core set of defined elements (or circumstances) whereby value can be created and encouraged for greater value-based progress. The four elements contained in this matrix were website value, user value, search engine value and business value.

Excessive process (within SEO delivery)

This relates to reliance on a set of repeatable actions beyond the point at which those combined steps become value enhancing. Excessive process is identifiable through a number of conditions including limited and restricted focus, and the frequent avoidance of change or development of strategy and tactics deployed for search engine optimization.

Technical health and maintenance (website)

From broken links and page loading time, through to content delivery, and the ability to facilitate website crawling and indexation. Technical health and maintenance is a means to benchmark, monitor and improve upon the total site's functional ability to support user and search engine ranking gains.

Website speed

Available for review at individual page level as well as at an aggregated total website level, site speed is the complete loading time (or average all page loading time) for a website. Site speed is a Google ranking factor contributing to search engine optimization improvement, and widely recognized as an important driving factor for both mobile and desktop user and search potential gains.

Website architecture

The architecture of a website is the way in which information is collected, displayed, organized and tagged (or labelled) in order to provide a logical order, hierarchy and access to the information (content) within the website.

Website navigation

A site navigation provides the visitors to a website with the textual and, or visual prompts, to logically (and when implemented successfully, intuitively) move around a website and access the most important content areas. Most sites have a number of navigational aids in addition to the most exhaustive 'main' or primary navigation.

Availability (website)

The proportion of the time that a website is 'available' is the percentage of the time the website is live and effectively loading out of 100 per cent for the duration of a year. The goal of website availability (also known as 'uptime') should be as high as possible – the ultimate target percentage being 100 per cent.

Search utopia

This is the desired situation where everything in your search marketing is perfect. Although in reality this is never totally achievable, knowing what the best situation looks like, enables you to strive towards various projected goals.

Key points

- Although 'value' has been a consistent point of reference throughout many of the previous topics covered, this book has not given you a practical guide for applying value comprehensively – until now.

- From experience, there are four key items that create a value-based checklist for search engine marketing: website value; user value; search engine value; and business value.

- Checklists themselves need to be regularly reviewed, refined and adapted, and this only becomes possible when you have a predictable level of questioning in place.

Building SEO expertise in-house vs outsourcing

LEARNING OUTCOMES

By the end of this chapter you will be able to debate and complete a decision-making process for either outsourcing SEO expertise or bringing SEO in house. You will know the most pertinent questions to ask (yourself or an agency) and create a decision tree to help lead to an SEO service provider outcome most suitable to you.

First, it is important to clarify what 'outsourcing' means. Put simply, outsourcing in this context refers to the action of employing the services of an external provider (most likely an agency, but this could also apply to a consultant or other form of specialist).

You can outsource part of a service or solution (in the area of SEO for example, you may outsource some elements like the analysis and recommendations, but opt to complete the implementation of the actions via your own developers), or outsource the service in its entirety. There can be advantages and disadvantages with both types of outsourcing, just as there are pros and cons to delivering SEO in house.

By contrast, in-house delivery is the delivery of a service without any direct external (or outside) support. It may be that you have existing internal resources for the servicing of SEO, or you may need new resources (staff) to fulfil the new requirement.

Questions you should ask

When a company, entrepreneur, or other entity, decides that they need search engine optimization services, one of the first and often initially challenging questions that they need to bring to an early conclusion is whether to employ SEO expertise in house or to use the services of an external agency, specialist or consultant.

This chapter should enable you to complete this process efficiently, without undue stress and for optimal value.

In this section we focus on asking the right questions.

As you might imagine, there is no set number of questions to ask, but in order to limit the required time and energy needed to obtain the core information required to make an effective business choice in this area, the most important questions to address are set out below.

Remember, these questions cover items to ask yourself, your staff and any external supplier. The questions you will ask and who those questions are directed towards will depend on your circumstances and requirements at the time, as will the weighting that you apply to the particular questions.

What is the initial cost?

Regardless of the end result, there will be an initial outlay or investment. When employing staff the initial costs may appear comparable to any fee charged by an agency, but it is important to understand that employing (often a single person) in-house is not a like-for-like comparison to employing an entire team (often the level of service required to support long-term results) within an agency environment. Having stated this, a single person working in your business will likely be able to provide capacity to the business in areas outside of any traditional agency service (usually these will be non-essential services, but still offering some perceived business value).

How much (ie what percentage) of a total marketing budget do you think should be set aside for search engine optimization?

What is the ongoing cost?

By its very nature SEO never ends. This is in part because of the aspect of earning results, as well as the ever-changing competitive and industry environment demanding ongoing expert attention. When you employ the services of a digital or specialist search agency (although I am referring to an agency, the same can be applied to individual consultants or other external resources), assuming the service remains the same (eg you do not add extra services, time or expert-driven support needs), then you can confidently expect the ongoing costs to remain fairly consistent.

With the creation of new roles within your business (or the expansion of current roles to service new specialist needs), the ongoing costs become less clear. As staff gain expertise, salary demands increase. Changing seasons, business requirements and competition may require additional resource, at least for the shorter term – it can be difficult to expand and reduce resources at short notice without external help. When looking at ongoing costs, it is necessary also to consider the ongoing returns on that cost. The investment returns from internal staff are noticeably different to those offered (in the main) by agencies; so, as with any investment, you will need to weigh up expected returns at this stage.

What level of expertise will we have access to?

Every person is unique, as are all agencies; but, when dealing with one of the fastest paced environments in a global marketplace, you need to have confidence that the people you are employing (directly or indirectly) are on top of their game.

If you are reliant upon a single person for everything SEO – here, I am referencing the fact that most initial in-house specialist SEO employment will at least commence with a single person rather than an entire team of experts – you are creating an added element of risk. Single-person delivery can make it difficult to remain self-challenged to keep up with the industry, self-scrutinizing, or being actively stimulated by a supportive search culture. An integral part of a digital agency is the enablement of daily innovation and improvement.

Part of this question covers the depth and breadth of access to expertise, as much as it does the overall quality. When working in an atmosphere of creativity and peer-to-peer knowledge sharing, it is more likely that expertise is nurtured more effectively and encouraged to blossom. While not impossible in-house, it certainly is more of a challenge.

> How will you objectively test the level of expertise you have access to, and how will you monitor this (and re-test) over the longer term?

How diversified is the experience of the staff?

When you work in-house you get the opportunity to immerse yourself in your business, your niche and your customer base. This can offer a number of advantages when it comes to understanding your audience, creating business marketing materials and delivering on brand media and PR in a timely fashion. Having a deep business understanding can become a competitive edge in its own right, but diversification of industry expertise can also open up new opportunities and support continuous momentum for longer term success.

Individuals can bring to the table a wealth of cross-industry knowledge in-house; however, the enormous breadth of experience obtained in an agency environment is unlikely to be rivalled when it comes to the potential gains from working on hundreds of campaigns, typical of many of the more established expert agencies.

As with all of these questions, there is a trade-off to be made, regardless of your current requirements. For highly niche and targeted businesses it may be more appealing to have very focused experience over a more diversified team's set of experience. For many other (more common) business niches, it is less likely that any single depth of niche experience would bring to the table a gain over the opportunity derived from the variety of experience spanning multi-niche expert working.

How integral will the people be to my business?

When you employ people in your organization, you invest in them. Assuming the investment is a sound one, it can be anticipated that the investment will return greater success to the business than the component parts of the service they provide. Examples of this may include how they add to your company's culture, the personal qualities they bring into the office each and every day (supporting other people and the company in wider areas than just those tied to their role) and much more. Although outsourced offerings may provide some of this non-service integral value, it is much more common to see these attributes within internal staff than outsourced staff.

How reliable is the service being delivered?

A core strength of an agency delivering a service (as with all these questions I am assuming a base level of professionalism) is consistency of approach. This stems from an assumption that the agency is good at what it does, and that it has a level of analysis in place for delivering a repeatable service that keeps up with the demands of the industry. Very specific training, development and assessment criteria are often in place in agencies, as are the opportunities to compare peer to peer, and provide the ongoing sharing of knowledge and expertise required to continue to deliver a professional service throughout the team and the company.

Regardless of how good an individual is in-house, you need to consider items such as sickness, holiday, personal development, attitude – reliance on a single person will produce highs and lows in both attitude and service delivered – and other areas such as longer term satisfaction, reward and periods of down time.

How long do I need to commit for?

I am challenging my own fundamental belief with this question, as SEO should never stop. However, for any business entity, it is a necessity to be able accurately to project and often limit any commitment. While some businesses can work effectively with short-term staffing contracts and higher levels of staff turnover, when recruiting genuine talent and specialism, you are not likely to attract (or keep) the best talent in this type of scenario.

By contrast, in an outsourced model, commitment will nearly always be defined from the outset. Contractual agreements will often include some form of duration commitment (whether long term or short term), and the important part of this is that it is clearly defined from the outset and all parties have agreed upon it. Having a defined commitment from all parties involved helps to focus attention, deliver results and maintain enthusiasm for the objectives in hand.

> What do you think is a *fair* amount of time to assess whether SEO being delivered is successful or not?

How do I get the right people on board?

Recruiting the right person for a new role, especially if the role itself is new to your business, is a difficult challenge. From creating the right job specification and asking the best questions at interview stages, to providing the training, support and development that the person will need to grow and maintain their skill sets – it is challenging to bring a new specialism into any business.

Going out to agencies can also be a daunting task. As SEO is a specialist niche, the task of interviewing agencies can increase the challenges of understanding what you need and cloud your ability to select the right agency for your business requirements.

Having said this, it is quite straightforward to review product offerings from the top agencies, retrieve very specific and tailored quotes, and speak to staff who are happy to avoid jargon from the outset.

Often a decision to go with an agency can be based, at least in part, on the people you meet at point of sale, and your experience of how successfully they understand you and your business, and address any questions you have (questions relating to the service, the industry or about the agency itself).

It is always a good idea to meet with your refined list of potential agencies in their offices, as this will enable you to discover more about the culture and the people behind the service.

How much control will I have?

When you decide to outsource, you are handing over at least a measure of control to another entity. By employing in-house, you opt to maintain full control over the staff and the delivery of the service. Whether or not keeping control is a positive will be specific to your situation.

One word of caution in this area, if you do decide to employ in-house, and controlling the service is seen as a benefit, you should exercise a degree of caution with regard to running the service directly. When you employ specialists, they need the ability to apply their trade and have ownership and accountability over a solid proportion of delivery.

Don't forget that outsourcing is usually a balance of involvement, collaboration and joint control. In many situations an agency will be happy to work with you to the level of involvement and control that best suits you, while also creating a mutually respectful environment that encourages the greater use of joint expertise (likely your industry/niche expertise combined with the agency specialist marketing expertise).

What does success look like?

This type of question helps to see how aspirational and realistic the people with whom you choose to work will be. Success appears different to every business and whatever path you take to fulfil your expert needs, it is important that you have people working with you. They must understand what you are looking to achieve, as well as having the ability to challenge (where appropriate) success measurements, and bring something additional to the party too.

> What measurements do you use to decide whether or not something is working for SEO?

How much time goes into research and development?

It is human nature to repeat what works and run with it. This can be efficient and deliver repeatable results. Everyone who has had success in any field of marketing, including digital, will recall the core components that created elements of success and creatively re-use them for longer term gains.

The main flaw with this is that the industry changes, competition evolves and tactics must also change accordingly. In an agency environment, the span of industries and campaigns worked on, as well as the level of peer expertise available for integrated working and creative thinking, sustains research and development. This R&D is put into evolving search marketing strategy, and provides long-term momentum for refinement of approaches and innovation. Agencies can take calculated risks, experiment and trial much more frequently than you would expect in house.

By contrast, and usually due to time commitments and the more generic nature of in-house working over agency specialism working, setting aside time for research and development can become an uphill battle. The level of research and development demanded for optimum service delivery needs prioritization for commitment over the longer term.

Are there any guarantees?

Yes. When someone asks if there are guarantees with SEO they are almost always told 'no'. There is good reason for this, which I will explain next; but for now let's cover why I said 'yes'.

When you employ a reputable, proven, thought-leading expert (whether internally or externally) you can guarantee that they will bring value to your website. You can guarantee that your content will be created on more than gut feel alone (data-driven content decision making), and you can be confident that your website will be technically better than it was when you started working with this expert.

Do not look for a guarantee of results – for example, in 'six months' time you are guaranteed a position in Google search engine results pages' (usually number one for a highly competitive small group of terms). If someone gives you a guarantee, you should avoid them at all costs.

You can be confident of potential agency performance from case studies, awards, time spent in the industry, telephone conversations with experts and other areas. When employing an individual you can gather some form of confidence from chatting to previous employers, looking at samples of their work and other items, though it is more difficult than building confidence in an agency.

What about link building?

Driving referral traffic to your website, encouraging brand awareness, and supporting general domain authority, links are a necessity for any SEO service. Very few companies (an exception may be one with a vast supplier chain or an unusually highly supportive external business network) have the ability to develop, run and consistently manage an effective link building campaign. Big brands do not count in this statement (big brands can be the exception to many rules and statements when it comes to search engine optimization), but most other companies do.

One of the reasons for this is that expert link building costs a lot of money, requires a large amount of contacts, or requires masses of time, resource and effort – often for non-guaranteed returns.

Links can pass votes of confidence, they can drive traffic, authority and sales, and can be a tangible return on investment. They can also cause adverse algorithm impact and manual penalties. This spectrum of challenge for link building means that in most situations you will need depth of expertise and likely a team of people assisting returns from time and money spent in this area of online performance.

How do you decide what to focus on?

Focus in this sense could be product ranges, keywords or anything else that is associated with your website. When people make a choice to start search engine optimization it opens up a breadth of opportunity and online aspiration that has otherwise gone relatively unnoticed.

An external agency will have a greater experience in the ability to contribute, and in many ways, lead the conversation in this type of discussion. Needing to prioritize between customers, campaigns and use of available expert resource every day, agencies can be highly effective at helping you select the right focus at the right time. An agency will be keen to demonstrate return on investment and progression generally. Getting the initial and ongoing focus right, is an important aspect of this.

In-house staff can of course also be very good at this. One of the added challenges of this 'however' for an internal team or expert, is that they are very much driven by the company line and key staff. More noticeable in small to medium-sized businesses where the board, founder, or other decision makers are still very much influential in all company strategy and decision making, is that it can be very difficult to suggest alternative approaches to focus when it is very apparent what matters most to the key people.

What's the risk?

There is some degree of risk with any decision, and deciding whether to stay in-house or to outsource SEO is no different.

When outsourcing, you need to pick the right agency for you. By looking at reviews, considering the age and reputation of the agency, and meeting the people delivering the service, you can mitigate a lot of this risk.

Reading the blog of the agency you are considering working with and picking up the phone, can be a great starting point, and an effective means to get a feel for the fit of the agency to your business. Asking to chat to satisfied customers can help you to discuss your feelings with people who have been through the same journey that you are on and who (most likely) feel that they have made the correct decision at the end of the process. This can be useful to address any outstanding fears over commitment to getting started. After all, the longer you delay any decision, the more ground you will have to make up on your online competition when you do get going.

Taking the step of recruiting also comes with some degree of risk. To a greater extent you will be concentrating all your requirements in a single person (as opposed to a likely team of experts with an agency) and expecting that person to be effective in a number of areas in addition to the delivery of the service alone.

For example; are they going to get on with other staff? Will they fit into your culture and add value to it? Are they reliable? How long will they remain with your company? How effective are they at SEO? What is their reputation for delivering results?

When recruiting, it can be more challenging to relay any outstanding fears and the person joining your business will probably also have a number of fears of their own to be overcome.

Does exclusivity matter?

When you add a new member to your team in-house, you are in effect adding someone to work exclusively with you. This gives you confidence that you have their full commitment and focus.

When working with an agency it is highly unlikely (unless you are an enterprise-scale business with a substantial budget) that you will have experts working solely on your websites marketing.

At this stage you will need to balance the gains of getting sole attention, over the potential value of broader expertise and experience. As with most, if not all of these questions, the answer is very rarely going to be a consistent one of win or loss for in-house staff or outsourcing, but more likely a question of what will work best in your current circumstances.

How much time is lost in translation?

When you outsource a service there will always be some time that is spent on explanation, repeat communication, travel and other areas. To a large extent this is mitigated with in-house working, although never completely removed. You could argue that time spent on explanation is also time used for education and therefore not a waste of effort, but that is very much down to the need to understand the business (understanding future time saving and business gains), or simply to understand what is going on (a short term and zero business time-saving item moving forward).

One of the workarounds for time *lost in translation* is outsourcing multiple services, so that they become an integrated and aligned multi-channel service.

A positive from this is that integrated working saves a lot of time. The experts are used to working together, and often the results that come from integrated working can far exceed the value derived from the delivery of the component parts in isolation. The negative aspect of this will mainly come back to the level of investment needed and business reliance on a third party.

Do you think that understanding what's being completed is as important as the end result derived from the actions?

Will expertise fade?

Expertise thrives when working with expertise. To remain on top of your specialism, you need to be challenged, able to debate ideas and spend time learning (constantly learning in fact). Agency life makes this process fairly simple (speaking from experiences I have had).

The challenge to remain at peak performance in-house is much greater. One of the primary reasons for this is the onus placed on the individual to self-motivate in this area, combined with the broader (and often non-specialist) extra duties that often form supplemental roles in-house (even more common in small to medium-sized businesses where everyone 'mucks in').

Employees in-house *are* the expert, so there is no peer-to-peer challenge, debate or frequent interaction to keep skills sharp. Human nature will lead to prioritization of time and one of the first things to be lost is the time needed to stay on top of the specialism.

The pace of industry change and development imposes a lot of time demands which, even if they slip for a few weeks, makes catching up a genuine barrier to commitment in this area of performance.

How do I know if SEO is working?

Many people may not feel comfortable asking this question, as the perception may be that there is a clear knowledge gap between the person asking this question and the people delivering the answer. This in fact, could not be further from the truth. Whether you opt for in-house SEO, or agency/outsourced SEO, you need to be clear about success and failure – how it is measured, what it looks like and how you will be kept in the loop on an ongoing basis.

From reporting, general communication and performance progress feedback, it is necessary to have clarity on this before you commit to a decision on your service provision.

If you are adding new staff to your team, they need to know whether they are doing a good job for you, so they will probably be as eager to have clarity on this point as you are.

An agency will want to create a profitable long-term relationship with you, and communicating effectively is crucial to achieving this. Both agency provision and in-house working will often result in some learning from both parties to get to a stage where it becomes easy to know how everything is going (and ideally without having to ask about it). However, I would expect an agency to be much more experienced in speeding up any learning and providing an initial structure to answer this from the outset (with refinements made as you collaborate along the way).

How many people will I need?

This question very rarely gets asked, but it is extremely important. The answer will vary depending on the scale of the project, the size of the business, the levels of competition in the market and many other factors. It is unlikely that a national campaign would be able to reach anywhere near its potential with search marketing if you are only looking at a single person delivering the project.

Many distinct specialisms come into play within a typical search engine optimization campaign including content, technical, social, development/design, creative, promotion and traditional SEO expertise. It is not likely that a single point of expertise would be *the* best person to provide all of these areas of specialist expertise.

A small business operating within a single place, or several locations, in a fairly non-competitive industry, could probably be served successfully by one person. At this point the challenge would be one of committing to employing someone full time or part time, or reducing this commitment to outsource the hours of one person to an external company.

How do we get the right content?

Search engine optimization does not work without content. This is not just about words on a page, but every type of content from organic advert, through to infographics and lots more. Content is so important to SEO success that it must be effectively fuelled throughout the strategy.

Do you have content writers? How do you decide what content to write? How frequently do you create content? What do you do with content once it has been created? What's the process for creating content? How do you share or promote content? How can you tell if the content you are creating is working?

These questions are just the starting point when it comes to content for websites, and generally supporting SEO success. You can outsource the content challenge to agencies, but of course there will be a cost associated to this. You can decide to create your own content, but then you need to justify the ability to commit the time, resources and likely costs associated with in-house delivery (and arguably the potential to produce the quality and quantities of content needed for an effective longer term online campaign).

> If you have worked in house for a significant period of time, how easy did you find it to set aside daily time for keeping on top of the industry? How did this type of task fit into your other priorities over the longer term?

Building vs outsourcing decision tree

Figure 7.1 gives you the main component parts of a decision tree which were covered in the previous section of this book. The point of giving you these elements in this form is that *you* can decide which items are important to your decision-making process, and which are less so (plus, which to ignore entirely, should you choose to).

A traditional decision tree leads you to a predicted set of end results based on assumptions of importance (pre-defined quantification of importance), and I do not believe this is as useful as it is letting you decide the weighting of these criteria for yourself.

Questioning the reasons behind actions, and avoiding overlooking logic due to pre-dictated assumptions, is something fundamental to this book, and the decision tree provided below – with the omission of predetermined decisions – remains true to this approach.

FIGURE 7.1   Building vs outsourcing decision tree

Choosing your SEO provider

1 Initial budget
Some level of budget will be required for any service addition. Budget smaller than minimum wage will leave agency only as the likely end decision.

2 Ongoing budget
Similar to initial budget, the minimum level of ongoing investment for new staff will likely exceed that of an agency.

3 Expertise level
In the majority of situations the level of expertise will be directly related to the budget available.

4 Experience diversity
Partly tied to level of expertise but, also driven by number of experts, access to volumes of campaigns and more. It is unlikely that in-house will rival agencies for diversification.

5 Integral to business
Traditional outsourcing by nature means that people working with you externally, are not as integral to the company (including in areas like culture) as an in-sourced person could be (certainly at outset), although longer term agency relationships do challenge this point.

6 Service reliability
Consistency of approach is likely to be more reliable with an agency, as opposed to an individual. The risk is likely to be higher when placing all requirements in this area on a single person over an external team.

7 Commitment
SEO should in most cases be considered a long-term commitment but it is likely that a company committing to new recruitment will be a longer-term decision than a company committing to a contractual minimum-service delivery time frame with an external agency. There will be exceptions to this.

8 Right people
The risk of getting the right people on board is more likely to be reduced when outsourcing compared to hiring in-house. This is even more so when recruiting for the first time for a new specialist role, mainly tied to the extra challenges during the decision-making process.

9 Control
Much more comprehensive control can be achieved through adding staff to your business. The additional question to consider, however, is whether the ability to exert complete control is a positive thing or not.

10 Success
Understanding success can be equally possible regardless of any internal or external resource available. The marginal potential added gain from agency services would be the valid questioning of success metrics, and the ability to apply experience from broader service-specific success measurements.

▶

FIGURE 7.1   *Continued*

11 Research and development
Repeating approaches that have previously driven results can be great for efficient working, however, long-term success demands that emphasis be placed on research and development. This is more likely to become a challenge in-house, although not an impossibility.

12 Guarantees
Access to performance information is easier and most likely more evident with agencies than it is with individuals during recruitment. A traditional guarantee is not possible for either in most cases, but supporting information to reduce the requirement for one, can be.

13 Link building
The spectrum of challenge for link building means that in a majority of situations you will need depth of expertise and likely a team of people to deliver link gains. While not impossible in-house, from experience, agency link building tends to be more successful over the longer term.

14 Focus
Effective focus can or course be achievable in-house, but agencies can be highly effective at helping you select the right focus at the right time, as well as offering an external challenge (when needed) to the status quo.

15 Risk
You will need to balance the gains of getting sole attention from recruiting in-house, over the potential value of broader expertise and experience from an external team. You will also have to question the actual value exclusivity brings to your bespoke needs.

16 Exclusivity
Outsourcing and in-sourcing carry risk. Either option carries a risk about the desired outcome.

17 Lost time
When you outsource a service there will always be some degree of time that is spent on explanation, repeat communication, travel and other areas. This is mitigated in most cases when recruiting in-house resources.

18 Fading expertise
Expertise thrives when working with expertise. To remain on top of your specialism, you need to be challenged, able to debate ideology, and spend time learning (constantly learning in fact). Agency life makes this process fairly simple, in-house less so in most cases.

19 Is SEO working?
Both agency provision and in-house working will often result in some learning from both parties to get to a stage where it becomes easy to know how everything is going; however, I would expect this process to be easier and more efficient with an agency (certainly to start with SEO as a new service to the business).

20 Number of people
Many distinct specialisms come into play within a typical search engine optimization campaign including; content, technical, social, development/ design, creative, promotion and traditional SEO expertise. How much of this you require will differ based on many variants.

21 Right content?
Content is so important to SEO success that it has to be effectively fuelled throughout the strategy. It is important honestly to consider the key questions about initial and ongoing content needs, and decide whether this is achievable best in-house or with outsourced support.

Key terms

SEO outsourcing

The business decision to supply search engine optimization expertise by means of using external service providers. Often part of the decision-making criteria for outsourcing specialist expertise is the reduced initial and ongoing costs. Outsourcing may be entire search solutions, and all areas of expertise required, or the supply of identified aspects of a wider, more comprehensive solution.

In-house expertise

In direct contrast to outsourcing expertise, in-house specialism relates to the acquisition of expertise to fulfil the requirements of a service without relying on external suppliers. This may include adding to the skill sets of current staff, or the addition to the organization of new expert staff.

Agency

Typically a search marketing, digital or other form of entity, an agency is the supplier of expert services required to deliver (in the context of this use) search engine marketing expertise. An agency has a number of roles including the primary one of matching expert resources to external business needs.

Consultant (search)

A specialist search marketing (SEO) professional able to provide expert advice based on knowledge gained in the field of search engine optimization (SEO).

Initial costs

The start-up or upfront fees required to commence a project (in this instance to start SEO services).

Ongoing costs

Operating fees, or continued outlay – this accounts for the repeatable costs (or fees) required to continue a service or maintain a level of service.

Link building

Link building, or link acquisition, relates to gaining or increasing external links (in its most common usage) in order to support search engine ranking factor gains as well as other desired outcomes, including referral traffic from one website to another.

Decision tree

A decision tree in its traditional form is a logical means to express a series of actions based on a predetermined set of possible choices. The underlying goal of a decision tree is to help problem solve a fixed number of alternative solutions by following a logical process of scenarios from start to finish. A decision tree can include a number of supplemental information items to help the user make progress through the required stages to ultimate final choice.

Key points

- When a company, an entrepreneur, or other entity, decides that they need search engine optimization services, one of the first, and often, initially challenging questions that they need to bring to an early conclusion, is whether to employ SEO expertise in-house or to use the services of an external agency, specialist or consultant.

- There is no set number of questions to ask; but in order to limit the required time and energy needed to find out the information needed to make an accurate choice in this area, the most important questions to contemplate have been provided in this chapter.

- Figure 7.1 gives you the main component parts of a decision tree as covered in the previous section of this book. The purpose of giving you these elements in this form is so that *you* can dictate which items are more important to your decision-making process, and which are less so (or which to ignore entirely, should you so decide).

Evaluating success in search marketing

LEARNING OUTCOMES

This section of the book is about evaluating success in search, putting in place meaningful measurements of success, looking at the bigger picture, and creating a longer term search marketing calendar. By the time you finish this chapter it will be easier to think about broader SEO and search opportunities. You will be able to look at search metrics specific to your own search objectives, and you can start creating your own long-term calendars for search marketing.

Restraint is one of the biggest limitations on search success. Restraint in terms of scope, creativity, and longer term planning, all impede the potential for greater gains through search engine marketing.

Thinking outside the medium

When you talk about search engine optimization in its current form, you significantly extend the traditional, and singular purpose, of maximizing the chances of search engines discovering and ranking your website (pages, domain and associated items) and start to consider the optimum performance of everything interacting with you, your business and your website online.

The focus that follows introduces 'SEO and ...'. The purpose of this is to show how SEO naturally overlaps and can effectively interact with, and improve, other forms of digital specialisms. While I have limited the scope of this type of medium enhancement to some specific areas (see list below) this could have been expanded to cover a number of additional items (eg SEO and User Experience (UX), SEO and e-mail, SEO and Conversion Rate Optimization (CRO)).

The intention here is to help you to expand your focus when it comes to search engine optimization so that is becomes instinctive to think outside of the medium.

At this point we consider:

- SEO and content;
- SEO and social media;
- SEO and PPC;
- SEO and design.

SEO and content

The most widely covered mutually beneficial digital relationship is between SEO and content. Every search engine optimization campaign requires the right type of content, and content cannot rely on quality alone for it to be seen by its intended audience.

Content creation

Before writing content you need to have a purpose and some degree of confidence that what you are writing has the chance of fulfilling that purpose. SEO places data at the centre of most decision making and this data-led mentality plus an expanse of access to data to drive decisions, supports effective content creation, outside of just 'content for SEO'. Content creation needs to be efficient and must span your entire audience information seeking and buying funnel. Content can be created to satisfy your audience needs, wants and desires, and nurture them from complete topic novices, right through to key educated decision makers. Your content should span all search verticals, offer something unique to the market, and differentiate you from your competition.

Content quality

Many ranking factors are tied to quality, and content quality is a fundamental minimum for any real chance of longer term SEO success. We are in a content age where more content is being produced than ever before, and a major driver behind this content creation is the need to succeed digitally. Producing the same quality content as everyone else is never going to be enough. Your basis for content creation needs to be 'better than everyone else' and substantially so. Many measurements can be linked to content quality including bounce rates, time on page, time on site, pages viewed, user interactions and engagement, sharing, syndication, and a myriad of other metrics.

Content keywords

Content needs to have clarity of topic. When we talk about content keywords, we are not looking at the secondary task of shoehorning keywords into content, but creating structured content around a logical theme. Keywords are the terms that you would expect to see in primary page headers, in supporting headings and within the most important elements of the page/copy that distinguish the body copy from any other page on the site. Keyword selection is paramount for helping content to be seen, rank well and reinforce user and search expectations. Keywords should be expansive (not restrictive) providing a structured depth of value far exceeding any small key term set being repeated for basic (dated) search engine manipulation tactics. Content keywords assist in user and search engine understanding, empowering easy content digestion, and confirming how and when content should be displayed for the right audience. You need to be using search terms that people actually use (coming back to the point made earlier about content not being able to rely on quality for visibility), include synonyms, term variations and regionality (where applicable).

Content originality

Whether you are looking at generating more *free* traffic, increasing brand awareness, protecting your site from negative algorithm impact (or manual penalties), or encouraging natural linking and social PR, you need fresh, unique, original content. Content originality exceeds the sole creation of content, and goes into the realms of thought leadership, opinion, newsworthiness and messaging. You should be repeatedly asking yourself 'what is missing?', 'what else can be said?' and questions like 'who is this content for?' As a content creator you have a duty to provide something interesting and meaningful.

Content optimization

To optimize something, you enhance it and make it better. For the purposes of search engine optimization of content, you make that content accessible to search engines and users. You make the content quick to load, clearly labelled and available in various formats, to cater for universal access to it. You ensure the content has depth of information, uses the right keywords, reflects expectations and has a clear topic. Content must be coded correctly, clear of errors, and must provide signals of intent to the visitor (whether human or robot). You review the data and learn from it, incrementally improving content, keeping it fresh and value added for the people digesting it. You make it easy to find, promote it and ensure it is having the desired impact (if it is not, you change it).

Content measurement

You need to measure the impact of content bringing it back to its original goals and purpose. A few questions that you might ask at this point include those below?

- Did the content fulfil what it set out to achieve?
- Did the content perform well in search?
- Did it rank highly for core themes and target phrases?
- How much traffic was driven to the site from the content?
- Did the content fuel goal completions/conversions or drive sales?
- Did users engage and interact with the content?
- How much reach did the content get?
- Did the right people see the content?
- How many links and social shares did the content get?
- How many landing page entries to the site came from this content?
- Did visitors to this content see other pages, spend much time on the site or just bounce?

SEO and social media

In this instance we are looking at SEO and free (as opposed to sponsored or paid) social media. It is widely acknowledged that social sharing, PR and general noise (or awareness) correlate strongly with contributing towards SEO success. Regardless of the social media platform, the greater the success derived from social media, often the quicker and broader the search gains also received. This relationship is not one of causation (ie strong social signals do not directly cause SEO success), but it is logical that social signals are a contributor to perceived content quality and value, something very much tied to successful SEO strategies.

Social discovery

Google uses every efficient avenue to locate new content and add it to the search index. As you might expect, content that is being widely engaged with, commented on and shared socially, is likely to be much easier to discover than content simply added to a site without any buzz surrounding it. When you consider that social media mixed content types like Twitter posts and YouTube videos are also included in many of the most prominent and competitive search engine results pages, the potential to leverage social media for content discovery is fairly substantial.

Social PR

While in many cases links from social media sites are 'nofollowed' (not passing direct authority from the social platform to the website being linked to), volumes of shares and interactions, combined with authoritative profile engagement, certainly offer indicators of content trust, quality, value and more. In addition to this, expanding the visibility and potential reach of content through social promotion will in many cases assist in traditional linking, in terms of people finding content they would not otherwise have been able to access.

Social content

Micro blogging platforms like Twitter and social media platforms generally, provide great real-time access to data. We previously discussed the importance of data in making decisions in content creation, and the additional of other data sources (in this case social media data sources) to encourage more meaningful data-led content creation. You also have the opportunity to collate unique user-generated information from polls, surveys and general social interaction and feedback that can lead to bespoke content construction. One of the main benefits from this type of content building is that you already know this is what the audience is looking for (as you have gathered direct data which tells you this is the case) and in many cases you have the right keywords (as it is user generated by your audience). These two areas are very strong signals that the content you develop will have a better likelihood of success in search.

Social repurposing

When you have gone to great lengths to produce industry-leading content, you want to make sure this content has a number of chances to succeed and provide repeat value over the longer term. By leveraging social channels (make sure that you go much further than just Twitter, Facebook, LinkedIn, YouTube, Pinterest etc) including many of the industry-specific social communities and future challengers to the mainstream channels, you can breathe fresh value into existing content. Through creative sharing, content segmentation and alternative content-type use of current information on your website, you can help fuel fresh discussion, interaction, search and user potential value, and a lot more besides.Many trends, user needs and solution requirements are cyclical. This means that the same content, when repurposed effectively, can provide repeatable and predictable ongoing value, far exceeding the initial impact when it first gets added to your site. Applying an SEO mentality to data-based refinement and innovation, you can confidently promote socially for expected returns on time and investment.

Social goals

As we proceed through these relationships with SEO, a common thread is the combination of objectives, goals and associated metrics that these distinct mediums all share. If you consider that common social media objectives include increased visibility/reach, user engagement, traffic and likely the end results from that traffic (micro and macro goal completions), all of these share commonality with SEO goals. A typical search strategy would look to leverage the potential value from many channels so that the overarching goals (items like traffic, goal completions, sales etc) are satisfied. While individual medium performance is still very important (as tailored approaches will be needed for improving each of them), if the ultimate objective is delivered, the contribution of multiple channels will nearly always exceed that of a single channel approach.

Social retail space

When you consider some of the more competitive search engine results pages (SERPs), those that are often dominated by a handful of the biggest global brands, sometimes one of the more feasible shorter term and initial avenues into these results is through alternative search channels like Twitter, Facebook, YouTube and so on. In addition to this, areas where your brand and business is especially strong will offer extra retail space to maximize for your own dominance. When you search for a brand (as one example of this in practice) you will be losing retail space if you do not have business accounts and active social involvement on all of the well-established, as well as the more niche social media platforms.

Social integrity

In this sense we are looking at integrity spanning a number of areas including provision of tangible value to your audience, solving problems with content, creating the right type of content that your audience needs, and using additional data sets (additional to SEO only data types) to create something unique to your business. The feedback in information available from social media can add a new aspect to your search marketing based on something much more meaningful that just a metric-based end goal.

Social immediacy

Gathering real-time data and leveraging real-time trends from social media can help your business be seen as an authority covering many core business areas. The power of brand, thought leadership and general domain authority can support many aspects of SEO success. If your business is repeatedly providing expert advice, opinion and general industry commentary earlier and more thoroughly than the competition, you can be confident (when your approach to SEO is supportive of digital performance) that this will lead to search marketing gains.

SEO and PPC

One of the most confused approaches to search engine marketing is the notion that one medium completes against another, or that, for one search channel to be a success, it has to be to the detriment of another. This simply is not true.

Part of this is likely to stem from search channel percentage share of total website traffic, conversions and other aggregated metrics. For example, if you are currently getting 25 per cent of your traffic from SEO and you increase this percentage share to 50 per cent, this does mean that the percentage share from other mediums will inevitably decline, *but* what is neglected is that the total numbers attributed may be much greater (ie 20 per cent of 2 million is far greater than 40 per cent of 10,000). From point of sale, through to repeat budget allocation, the spend levels on one medium should very rarely take from another – how many times have you been involved in conversations that include the question 'should we invest in SEO or PPC?' In almost every scenario, the reply should be 'both'.

Paid data

The removal of the bulk of organic, post-click keyword data from Google has been one of the biggest game changers (actually on balance a very positive one) for the SEO industry. With paid data, you can plug many of the data gaps left by 'not provided' data from Google. Keywords are massively important to decision making and the more data you can collate, the better.

Keyword data can offer paid and organic actions as well as aligned tactics and strategy creation, unavailable when working with either medium in isolation.

Paid promotion

Getting the right content in front of the right audience as frequently as possible, is a primary goal for SEO, PPC and most other digital marketing mediums. When you start to use the benefits of one (or many) distinct mediums to leverage their combined value, and overcome their individual restraints, the potential extra proposition can be vastly increased. As one example, consider the extra gains of re-marketing content (remarketing basically being a paid option to display repeated advertising on external websites once a user has visited content on your site) that you know performs well with your current audience, and targeting it to the same personas in new areas (relevant external websites) unavailable to your business historically. Think about the added brand gains, social signals and broader search engine authority that can come as secondary benefits from this paid promotion and remarketing.

Paid audience

Searchers have learnt habits when it comes to their search engine use and behaviour. Some people will click on paid adverts over organic, as it can be a signal of buying power and indications of trusted service expectations. Other searchers will opt for organic (or natural, free or earned) results, as they cannot be bought. SEO adverts can convey relevancy, authority to search and perceived value to be gained when landing on high-ranking websites. The fact is, if you are not in the highest positions, most frequently on both paid and organic retail space, you are losing out on business. The more you can mitigate this loss through high performance in both SEO and PPC spanning all effective visibility areas, the greater the cumulative business returns will be.

Paid page one

Most user clicks occur on page one of search engines. The more you can appear on page one, the greater the percentage share of the total available clicks (traffic) your business will receive. At its most basic form, this click maximization lies at the heart of SEO and PPC collective contribution towards aligned search engine marketing success. Increased page one visibility and business exposure supports greater click-through rates (CTR), trust, traffic and ultimately sales (conversions) from search.

Paid scoring

When you advertise on paid media through Google your content/pages/keywords receive a quality score. This score tells you how relevant, and valuable you rank in these areas. Higher quality scores lead to lower cost per clicks and as such, leveraging SEO to improve your content/pages/ keywords and entire site scoring will reduce the paid spend needed to bid to the same positions. This potential aligned reward and direct saving can be a great motivator for businesses *toe dipping* into SEO for the first time.

Paid ceilings

Some keywords are not feasible to some businesses to make a return in investment. As an example, if your profit margin on any given product is less than your competition, and you both bid to your maximum effective levels, you will not be able effectively to outbid them over the longer term. By using SEO to target non-feasible PPC terms, and PPC to gather data and fuel decision making on longer term SEO keywords, you can overcome key limitations placed by one medium with the benefits and success of another. This limitation solving through multi-channel marketing is something you will notice repeatedly mentioned in this section of the book.

Paid optimization

PPC campaigns can derive a great amount of campaign management value from SEO best practice (consider tactics used for SEO content themes and the set-up and structure of paid ad groups), and SEO (notably technical on page SEO) can drive a lot of value from paid keyword data and more. The extra optimization actions that can be directly incorporated by transferring the logic from one channel to another can make the difference between gaining or losing ground online. At a more granular level, actions like advert updates (title tags and meta descriptions) can be directly transferrable (or at a minimum logic transferrable) from one channel to another – again, for the purposes of improvement and refinement.

Paid attribution

Attribution in this context simply relates to being able to associate an end result (attribute it) to a medium. In Google Analytics and other data solutions, you can see how multiple channels interact to deliver an end result. From first click attribution (the user's first interaction receiving all of the end result accrediting) to last click attribution, and any click attribution, it is clear that digital channels are not performing in isolation, they are all contributing, interacting and working together. As an example of this, a user may click on a story you have published on your website which has been include in Google News. They spend 30 seconds skim reading your content and close down their browser window. The news section of your website has paid re-marketing in place. As that user visits other related websites a week later, they see your banner advert appearing. They go onto Google and type your brand name, as they begin to increase their interest in the wider company, outside of just the initial story that attracted their interest in the first place (a story which may no longer be of interest to them). They go to your home page and bookmark it. Three days later they use that bookmark to buy something from you. Direct traffic would gain the last click attribution; SEO would gain first click attribution; and any of these mediums could claim 'any click attribution'.

Paid reputation

When dealing with reputation management your initial concern and focus area is on reducing the visibility of any negative PR by pushing the information as far away from the top of the search results as possible. The most effective way to achieve this goal is by combining SEO, PPC, social media and a host of search engine visibility opportunities to maximize your desired coverage.

SEO and design

If you have worked on a number of SEO projects including website re-designs and new website builds and launches, you will no doubt have been in situations where design and SEO are in conflict. There is very good reason for this, as some of the roles and deliverables from design briefs are very different to those of an SEO campaign.

However, SEO and design have many aligned and overlapping goals, and they rely on each other to deliver more successful end results. If you can focus on the aligned goals, and effectively communicate the needs behind any conflicting website objectives, you will find that the end result delivered from a collaborative SEO and design relationship will deliver greater returns from your investment.

Next we discuss some of the common opportunities and strengths of a combined SEO and design approach towards websites.

Mobile friendly

Since the launch of the Google mobile update, and the inclusion of mobile friendliness as a ranking factor, design and SEO experts have been working together to ensure that any website design and associated content are effectively being digested on mobile devices. Mobile responsiveness, the re-organization of content and page elements, and general mobile friendliness (the ability for people to engage and interact with your content on smaller screen resolutions, mobile devices and tablets) are shared responsibilities of website projects with SEO and design working together to deliver the right solution.

Page and site speed

Having a great-looking website will help to convey important business quality and trust signals. Effective design can help one website stand out from the next and lead the user smoothly through your website. Designs that are predominantly image based and rich with multimedia can, however, emphasize look and feel to the detriment of user and search experience. This is something to be avoided at all costs, if you are going to convert the people that discover your website, or drive volumes of free traffic to your website in the first place. Balancing site performance (in this case speed) with design, is an ongoing area requiring the effective working of both SEO and design. Images can be compressed without loss of quality and mixed media made web ready. Page and site speed is a ranking factor, so directly tied towards search engine ranking results, as well as a key factor for delivering a positive user experience.

Content optimization

Website templates have to include a number of layers of SEO value in order to support potential gains whenever you add new pages of content to your site. Some of the most frequently overlooked items in website items that can directly impede a site's ability to perform well in search include the following:

Header tags control

Ability to add, update and change page headings without changing other site aspects. For example adding an h1 tag or h2 tag without this changing the page title tag, the breadcrumb navigation, or other sub-navigation or menu items.

Title tags control

A title tag controls the top section of your organic advert, so controlling this can be critical for refining and improving click-through rate gains, including the right keywords to support ranking gains, and to show page theme and relevance from the search engine results pages (SERPs) right through to the user landing on your web page.

Meta descriptions control

Paired with the title tag, the meta description helps to drive traffic (clicks) to your website from visibility (impressions in the SERPs). You want total control of meta descriptions, so that you can monitor, update and improve how much value you are getting from your organic adverts appearing. It can be useful to have the ability to apply rules (data to be populated by setting specific criteria) to populating meta descriptions as well as (and this is the important part) the ability to manually override and update them. A large e-commerce website for example, may have thousands of pages, so initially you may want to populate meta data with certain content form known database tags. As an example you may wish to include product names, prices, free delivery message and more. You will also want to be able to make sure that the content is well written, engages the user, and includes a relevant call to action – to make the user click now!

Site architecture

Design, SEO and usability, all need to work hand in hand to produce an initial website design that is intuitive, reflective of the business hierarchy, and enables effective content discovery, crawling and indexation. Regardless of the industry and how design heavy a website may be (there are a number of logical reasons for why a specific website may choose to be design orientated over content or user orientated), the site architecture needs to work effectively for the user and the business and for search engine success. SEO experts have an important role when it comes to balancing the needs of the user, the business, and search engines. In many situations the role of your SEO expert (or consultant) can often include balancing the demands of disparate and competing website needs and getting the right end result.

Accessibility

In part this goes back to one of the fundamental principles of search engine marketing – that is, information needs to be accessible and available universally, regardless of location, time of the day, day of the week, month of the year. Whether users have a fast internet connection or a slow one, are using an iPhone or an Apple Mac, they should be able easily to access and digest your site content. The same principle applies to people with other specific needs, for example, people with visual impairments, who need the ability to read the screen, or more accurately, listen to it. There are a number of technical SEO factors that need to be in place to support effective understanding of content using screen readers and other devices. When you have amazing visuals, SEO can work with design to help them to be understood, discovered and placed before the right people at the right time. There is very little point in creating industry-leading visuals if they are seen by only a tiny minority of your potential online audience.

Social sharing

We are probably spanning several specialism here (SEO, design, social media, and potentially PR), but the concept remains the same – experts need to work together in order to maximize and leverage the value of what is being created when it comes to websites. There is strong correlation between social PR, content sharing and general social media buzz and search engine results. Content that is shared by the right influencers and volumes of genuine social media profiles gets found quicker, will have greater content quality signals and encourage ranking gains. When users can engage with interesting designs and enjoy expert design elements, including content types, an initial reaction is to share it. Facilitating content sharing, embedding into external sites and general user engagement, all help to improve the value derived from the expert content created.

Content understanding

There are a number of ways in which professional SEO practitioners can apply their expertise to help search engines like Google understand content more effectively. One of the first stages of creating effective content is enabling search engines to find it, and next, understand it. From surrounding content to technical SEO updates and code additions, there are many ways to help content understanding without any detriment to design, look and feel of a web page. As one example of this, images can include titles and alt tags so that search engines can receive text descriptions of the content. Naming files is also an important factor for image optimization and general search engine context and understanding. This type of activity can be put into a sample process so you can see how this might work in practice with SEO and design working together. It is important to understand that this is just an example process; the actual process will differ based on many unique circumstances.

- SEO expert identifies an opportunity to increase content value on an existing blog web page (increase initial value notably in image search verticals but also the perceived quality value by incorporating mixed content types for the user and segmenting of content).

- Design expert talks through the intended results of the new images with the SEO expert and creates three new visuals.

- SEO expert names the images so they are relevant. At the same time, as they get added to the blog page, the SEO expert adds a title tag and image alt text so that search engines and users have greater context about what is contained within the images.

- Once the images have been live for a few days, the SEO expert analyses the latest data and sees that users are hovering over the images with their mouse, but at present they are static, so the user cannot gather next stages of value.

- Working with design, the SEO expert has the images updated so that when a user hovers over them, they are presented with new content. This is styled overlay content which only appears when a user hovers their mouse over the image. Then content gives the user (and through the code, search engines) more information about the images and includes a call to action per image, so that the user can learn more about buying this product (in this example the images are products that have been mentioned in a blog post).

- The design expert further refines the image overlay (and in this case image on hover actions) value by changing the colour of the secondary content the user sees when they mouse over the image. The colour stands out from the rest of the template as it is not part of the standard template colour palette. After the update it is clear in the data that users are now not only hovering over images, but also clicking on them and landing on product purchasing pages.

- The SEO experts refine the content displayed and the call to action several times until they are satisfied that the image is driving the optimum level of internal page views to the product pages from this blog.

- The end result is that through design and SEO working together, they have created increased revenue from existing website traffic. This would not have been achieved without collaborative, cross-expertise working.

Breadcrumb navigation

Although not a requirement for every website, it is worth considering whether you website would benefit the user and search engine results with the inclusion of a breadcrumb navigation. Usually situated at the top of the page below the main navigation (although in theory it could easily be placed in other elements of the page and site template), a breadcrumb navigation can provide a number of positives to a website design. A few of these benefits are as follows:

- Users and search engines can understand where content sits within the broader site. For example; Home>Office>Stationery>Pencils>Blue Pencil – in this example I can see that the current page ('Blue Pencil') sits within the pencils sub-section of the site. I can click on this and widen the scope of other pencil types and colours. If I wanted, I could further expand my focus to all office stationery (by clicking on 'Stationery' in the breadcrumb navigation). Here I could add a number of products to my order (assuming this is in an e-commerce website environment) which provides a more efficient user, business, and search experience, saving time and repeated searching for end results. As a user I could also use the breadcrumb navigation for further search filter refinement (going to the 'Office' section), or I could go back to the website root (the home page –'Home').

- Visitors to your sites can have single-click access to more of your website. This facilitates easy information access, quicker user journeys (and completion of their intended outcomes from landing on your site) and refine their interactions with your site. Through effective search engine optimization website visitors should be landing on the most relevant pages and content on your site match to their search query; however, this is not always the case. Breadcrumbs can help users get back on track with their information seeking and buying.

- Breadcrumbs are by nature quite intuitive. This means that the user has a greater perception of their ability to interact with and engage with your website. Removing barriers between the user and the website and encouraging easier navigation is fundamental to improving user-quality signals and website conversions from your audience.

- When marked up correctly with the right coding, breadcrumbs can appear as 'rich snippets' in Google search engine results pages. This can tell you two things. First, Google places value on the use of breadcrumbs – so much so, that it is including some of their functionality and value in its search results. Second, the user will gain from understanding more about the context of content (see previous the first bullet above) and this will help them decide whether to click on your advert. Any means whereby you can derive greater value from current visibility is important for making the most out of search opportunity.

- Breadcrumb navigations are unobtrusive and deliver minimum impact on design. This means that you are able to generate more value for search engine success and for the user, with few if any negative factors to consider. Any search and user tactics where there are few if any potential downsides must be seen as primary tactics to deploy.

- Effective breadcrumb navigations help seed important terms on pages. Some pages on your website will have limited standalone value. While you should always strive to have a content rich and high user experience on every page accessible by users and search engines, form the outset this is unlikely to be the case. When you can leverage the template of the website more effectively (breadcrumbs are one example of this), you are building into the site a repeatable and automated value added. Any ways in which you can help new pages have a better chance of being understood, add value to the user and support SEO wins, are important for continuous and consistent performance.

Search metrics that matter

When we start to consider measurements for SEO success (or metrics that matter), what is most important is identifying what matters most to you and your business. While all digital marketing mediums bring traditional measurements of success, these should not be taken as the only, or the most relevant, metrics to measure your own evaluation of performance.

I want you to think about what you want to achieve and then reverse engineer this into the metrics required to gauge whether your SEO tactics and strategy deployed were a success or not. The achievement areas focused on in this section are some of the more commonly targeted metric groupings. This is by no means an exhaustive list, but it will provide some starting inspiration:

Quality

There is always some degree of balancing between quality and quantity when it comes to measuring the effectiveness of search engine optimization. The ideal situation is that you get more volume and higher quality; however, it can be helpful to distinguish the two for tailored SEO strategy creation and delivery. Part of this is that the two can be competing and contrasting in approach – meaning that collating them into a single approach will often lead to decision making that is counterproductive in terms of one (quality) or the other (quantity/volume).

Example quality metrics include:

- Click-through rate (CTR) – the number of clicks (expressed as a percentage) compared to the number of times your organic advert has appeared (impressions).

- Bounce rate – the percentage of people who leave (exit or bounce) from your website after only visiting a single page. In many cases the lower the bounce rate, the better; but there can be exceptions to this rule.

- Time spent on page/site – every website will have different optimum user time on page (or site). Generally, the longer people spend on your web page or site, the better; however, there will be a point at which you will want the visitor to complete an end goal, meaning that exiting the site is a logical and necessary conversion step.

- Visibility and traffic relevancy – it is one thing increasing impressions and footfall to a website, but another thing to ensure that it is effective (relevant and likely to convert).

- User engagement – this can include many items and helps to understand how active and interested the people landing on your website are. This may be people downloading forms, watching videos, or a myriad of other areas.

- Pages seen per visit – as a measurement of quality, this can tell you if visitors to the site are digging deeper into your offering. If you have a minimum number of steps or pages required for an end result (eg a financial services company may require reading of terms and conditions, key features or other page content prior to completing an application form), the pages/visit measurement will be important.

- Demographics – including language and location. Most businesses will have a target audience tied to location as well as language. Matching traffic received as closely as possible to this is a useful quality assessment criteria. If for example, you sell female-only product ranges specific to over 60s, other demographic data that you would be looking at tied to demographics would include gender and age.

- End results – what is the final action you want a user to complete? The higher the percentage of impressions or visits to this end result the better. For e-commerce websites this would include conversion rates, transactions, abandonment rates, and revenue. For non-ecommerce websites, this could include goal conversion rates, event completions and more. Do not overlook how much assistance is provided (eg assisted conversions show how marketing channels interact in order to deliver an end result ignoring a single attribution of decision making).

- Channel comparison – applicable to pretty much every metric, performance of one marketing medium to another can be a great sign of quality.

- Price of keyword – this is slightly more creative than many quality metrics, but it is something I really like, as it can help see the value of quality. When you compare the traffic you are receiving based on CTR and number of impressions you are appearing for, you can have an estimate of clicks/traffic and times this by the 'suggested bid' from Google Keyword planner, or CPC from your AdWords data, if you are running PPC campaigns as well (or any other external tool which provides an average value per keyword). As Google paid models are auction based, this means the higher quality terms (assuming relevancy) will be those requiring the highest bid (or showing the highest average price/suggested bid).

- Value delivered – do not underestimate the quality that can be attributed by reflecting and measuring the perceived value that you have provided to your target audience. This has many forms of measurement including shares, social engagement and interaction, backlinks (natural linking), direct feedback, and more.

Volume (or quantity)

As you might expect, when referencing volume, we are simply stating 'let's focus on increasing xyz' as an area of return from investment into SEO. Volume-based metrics can be anything, so the following list includes a few measurements, and I would recommend that you look at volume goals spanning not only the final end result, but every contributing micro step that is required to support that end result.

Example quantity metrics include:

- Impressions and traffic – being seen more in the right areas (effective impressions) and turning this visibility into people landing on your website (traffic).

- Topics and themes – increasing the number of relevant topic areas in which you are seen as an authority will support almost all other metric increase focus areas.

- Rankings and average positions – improving the quantity of top position rankings and average positions supports visibility, brand awareness and many other associated measures of progress.

- End results – as covered in the above section (including ROI and micro goal completions).

- Page and section attention – this can include landing page/section impressions, traffic and results. This can also include improvements in visibility and engagement with these pages/sections after visitors are already on your website (driving more people to the most important areas of your website regardless of their current position).

- Amount saved – in this case I am referring to the potential cost of the traffic had it been paid for through paid search. See 'price of keyword' in the previous section, for detail on this metric.

- Percentage contributed to total site success – this could be tied to traffic, conversions, goal completions, or any other metric. What we are looking at is taking a benchmark of how much of 'metric x' comes from SEO at present compared to the rest of the tracked mediums and then increasing it (eg at present you may get 45 per cent of total website visits from SEO; increasing this to 55 per cent would be a 'percentage contributed to total site success' measurement).

- Customer acquisition cost – increasing the volume of active customers reduces the cost of acquiring them. The ability to generate more active customers at a lower acquisition cost can be fundamental in website and broader business success.

Technical and performance

This is perhaps one of the most frequently neglected measurement groupings for SEO performance and results, but it supports most other measurements of success.

Example technical and general website performance metrics include:

- Accessibility – consider all of the items that make your content, messaging and website pages universally available without exception.

- Access to data – gathering of data specific to your website is imperative for technical and website performance benchmarking and improvement. This includes availability, breadth and depth of data available to you, as well as the integrity of the data itself for deriving meaning and insight.

- Site speed – including mobile, device and desktop. The faster your website performs, the better the experience it delivers, and the more potential quality perception is present to support mobile and other device search engine performance.

- Operability and functionality – including redundancy to actively trying to break the website. From broken pages and content, through to access to information needed.

- Uptime – the amount of time that your website is available for purpose. The digital environment is active 24 hours a day, seven days a week and 365 days a year, every year.

- Search appearance – in this case looking at the core elements of Google Search Console (GSC), (formerly Google Webmaster Tools (GWT)) criteria including HTML improvement areas and more.

- Usability – how intuitive the site is and how friendly it appears to be to the people using it.

- Natural linkability – in this example we are considering the quality and quantity of backlinks being created without any intervention other than what you add to your website. It is unusual to include this in a technical area of website review, but when you include broader website performance measurements, I do not feel this can be excluded.

- On-page support – traditional on-page SEO analysis, auditing, benchmarking and improving.

- Off-page support – likely to include a degree of SWOT (strength, weakness, opportunity and threat) analysis as well as analysis, auditing, benchmarking and improving.

- Redundancy to impact – to hacking, and other external negative influencers (including Google negative algorithm impact and manual penalties).

- Search supportive – ability to encourage effective crawling and indexation of content, understanding of the website and removal of any technical impediments to search engine success.

- Volume of site indexed – tied in part to the above 'search supportive' point; however, the measurement is simply how much of the website you intend to be indexed and deriving some degree of search value that is actually being delivered or achieved.

- Hierarchy and architecture – is the website logically structured? Is the most important content clearly distinguished and more prominent than the remainder of the site's content? Can all indexable content be discovered by users and search engines?

- Mobile site success – Does the site technically perform in mobile search? Is the site mobile friendly? How much of the site's success comes from mobile search? These, and other questions form the basis for measurement of success in this area.

- Content delivery – This will also touch upon other areas mentioned including speed, on-page support and more, as well as quality measurements (both positive ie engagement and sharing and negative ie duplication, thin value).

- Internal information access – Aka 'internal linking'. Can users and search engines discover associated content without the need to use the main or supportive navigation elements of the website? Is there depth of access to information on a topic and theme? How natural and intuitive is the linking? This is really a very brief introduction to a much broader are of focus.

Creating your longer term search calendar

This part of the chapter focuses on the need to diarize important calendar events to support search marketing success. This reflects the importance of SEO and content working together, and includes references to broader topics than a content or editorial calendar would do in most instances.

In this context, a 'longer term search' calendar incorporates the core content delivery elements required to support an effective SEO campaign. As with many of these areas, this is not an all-inclusive list of SEO content calendar approaches, but it includes some of those which can be effective in fuelling creativity in this area.

Where useful, calendar examples have been provided – the purpose of these is to reinforce the practical application of this approach.

Before we go into the practical examples it is important to remove some of the barriers that can crop up before companies are able to allocate time to search calendars. The following are some of the frequently asked questions that can cause barriers to search and content calendar creation:

- Why create search marketing calendars?

- What are the key objectives of search and content marketing calendars?

- Where's all this new content going to go?

Why create search marketing calendars?

There are many ways to approach this question, but an important part of the justification process relates to planning, consideration and execution. When you create a single point of reference for all parties to use, you provide a visible resource to plan a content-based (or certainly a content-supportive) search marketing strategy.

When you have an inclusive means to identify who is doing what, you are able to question, prioritize and enhance it. This review (or consideration stage) is where the data analyst trait of the SEO expert combines with the creativity of the content marketer to apply added meaning within the longer term search calendar creation.

The execution phase includes recording what was (or was not delivered) to schedule, what initial impact can be seen (this impact analysis is useful for refinement, next phase prioritization, improvement and more) plus, any insights, next steps or changes to the search marketing calendar from the execution of scheduled content.

What are the key objectives from search and content marketing calendars?

One of the prominent areas in answering this question is links to making integrated working easier and more effective. It is difficult to question the value of combining expertise for greater expected return; but facilitating effective working is another topic altogether.

Some of the main additional expected returns from implementing SEO and wider search calendars like this include:

- having clear consideration points to assess what you are planning to do and why;
- documented strategy, planned tactics and the opportunity to compare your schedule activity and the external environment (historical/ current/future) strengths, weaknesses, opportunities and threats;
- prioritization of available resources based on expected return (likely metrics and value-based returns over traditional ROI) for key content needs (likely search strategy plus content);
- expansion of content, refining of approach, and identification of any new opportunities far in advance of content needs;

- easy publishing and clear processes for implementation. What is often overlooked is making live, operability testing and the next-step processes of what happens before, during and after new content goes live. Consider items such as promotion, social sharing, influencer updates, key staff engagement etc.

> What are the key areas you would include in your longer term search calendar – and why?

Where's all this new content going to go?

Every new item of content you create must have a defined purpose. If all of the content you produce is going on your website you will be missing out on many external opportunities to deliver search success. If all of your content is going externally, your website is likely suffering, and most of your time and energy is supporting other people's website successes online.

The same piece of content may exist in many forms and service a number of purposes; for example, a survey may be segmented and used for social media questions, thought leader engagement and to continue conversation. The same survey could likely be included in an on-site blog post or expert opinion piece (or a series of on-site posts).

Data from the survey may be used in external forums to answer questions relevant to your audience to help with brand awareness and genuine business value, or perhaps in valid comment placement within mainstream highly trusted media and PR sites.

Textual data may then be repurposed into more creative content types like presentation slides, short expert videos and infographics.

The actual decision for content placement should be concluded early on, well in advance of any content actually being created. One of the reasons for this is that content destination needs to reflect the style, type and pitch of the content you develop. Doing this retrospectively is not a suitable tactic for effective time, resource or expertise management.

> How effective have your content placement or website implementation tactics been to support your SEO goals?

Monthly search calendar

Do not over-complicate your longer term search calendars – you want information to be accessible for everyone involved, easy to use and understand, and effective to manage and to maximize for search marketing success.

If you are creating your search calendar in Excel, Excel Online, or other similar office-based applications, you may want to segment granularity based on audience, ease of understanding, or other meaningful criteria.

The following monthly search calendar is objective based and gives you some ideas of the type of objectives and tactics in force before you attribute content to the calendar to achieve those objectives.

> Setting and restricting available space to enter information into a search calendar requires some form of quality control at the point of entry. This is great for maximizing focus on objectives only.

TABLE 8.1   Monthly search calendar – objectives based

KEY:

O is objective (in this case just one overarching objective and in this instance it changes monthly for variation in the examples provided. In reality objectives will coincide, often over many months).

T is tactic (a handful of relevant actions tied to the objective. These are some relevant tactics to reflect a much broader set of actionable insights likely to be deployed).

Jan	Feb	Mar
O: Increase traffic	O: Improve traffic quality	O: Generate conversions
T: Add weekly content to blog	T: Survey audience needs	T: Create persona-driven content (target bottom of funnel)
T: Promote snippets socially	T: A/B test content variations	
T: Repurpose existing content	T: Review blog conversion data	T: Provide seasonal discounts and promote
T: Leverage newsworthy stories	T: Prioritize landing pages content additions	
T: Expand the content depth on key pages		T: Create comparison content for product/service pages

Apr	May	Jun
O: Increase brand awareness	O: Increase rankings on products	O: Increase effective traffic
T: Actively push content through social PR		T: Use five previous months of data to drive effective content creation
	T: Add user-generated content to product pages	
T: Create guides/linkable assets and promote	T: Increase the depth of content on category level landing pages	T: Revisit most successful blogs and refresh/update/re-promote
T: Create content that solves problems and push out to forums, social media, on-site FAQs and mixed content type offerings	T: Add structured data to product pages including review code	T: Repurpose guides into visual content, share and promote
T: Engage with industry events		T: Target another search vertical ie video or news, by creating mixed content

TABLE 8.1 *Continued*

Jul	Aug	Sep
O: Increase mobile success	O: Become more visible online	O: Educate my audience
T: Update your website to include responsive design functionality	T: Expand all core, top-level pages' content	T: Create top of funnel (catch-all) content to peak interest
T: Improve desktop and mobile site speed	T: Complete on-site technical SEO	T: Build and nurture social channels for repeat debate
T: Re-prioritise content order and placement on the page	T: Update pre-click optimization areas (title tags etc)	T: Offer free advice and opinion on respected external websites
T: Complete mobile-friendly actions	T: Add new services, products and content variety to the website (find more content that is missing at present)	T: Create something new, unique (needed by your audience) and likely based on data you have collected
		T: Provide free webinars

Oct	Nov	Dec
O: Improve domain authority	O: Refresh existing content	O: Leverage ROI
T: Build relevant business links	T: Identify and improve lowest performing pages	T: Gather more data (ie add call tracking or new data collection items)
T: Promote content and generate social 'buzz'	T: Add fresh content to old, but relevant content pages	T: Provide new testimonial/ review/case study content
T: Remove low-quality links and replace with higher value backlinks	T: Create 'roll-up' content for fresh link signals to existing pages	T: Complete conversion rate optimization
T: Re-visit technical SEO	T: Complete new keyword research and update term frequency, placement and variation	T: Add new upsell content and cross-sell details to key product pages
T: Improve internal linking		T: Improve your product images
T: Add more linkable assets to the site (natural linking content features)	T: Include commonly asked questions and answers pertinent to the page content: expanding value and depth of topics covered	T: Complete image optimization
T: Improve pages which have thin content or that are not contributing enough to total site success		T: Add more surrounding content to pages

Weekly search calendar

At this stage we add another level of granularity to the longer term search calendar. At a weekly level, tactics will require specific content creation and actions competing, and need assignment from creation to implementation.

Table 8.2 shows a single week example for the purposes of illustration – the focus of this calendar is effectively to manage search content workload.

TABLE 8.2 Weekly search calendar – managing workload

In this case the focus is on visibility of information, allocation of task and prioritization of completion.

Completion date	Priority	Assigned to	Objective	Task type	Task	Location (on-site, off-site) + URL	Impact after 30 days (data changes tied to objective)	Next action (detail)	Next action (date)	Next action (assigned to)
03/10/2016	High	Jane	Increase traffic to 'x' section	Technical SEO	Link to full brief	URL	URL	TBC – post-data review	TBC – post-action identified	TBC – based on skill set needed and resource availability
03/10/2016	Low	Jane	Increase traffic to 'x' section	Content	Link to full brief	URL	URL	TBC – post-data review	TBC – post-action identified	TBC – based on skill set needed and resource availability
04/10/2016	Medium	Bob	Increase traffic to 'x' section	Content	Link to full brief	URL	URL	TBC – post-data review	TBC – post-action identified	TBC – based on skill set needed and resource availability
04/10/2016	High	Bob	Increase traffic to 'x' section	Content	Link to full brief	URL	URL	TBC – post-data review	TBC – post-action identified	TBC – based on skill set needed and resource availability
05/10/2016	Low	Russell	Increase traffic to 'x' section	On-page SEO	Link to full brief	URL	URL	TBC – post-data review	TBC – post-action identified	TBC – based on skill set needed and resource availability
05/10/2016	Medium	Bob	Increase traffic to 'x' section	Pre-click optimization	Link to full brief	URL	URL	TBC – post-data review	TBC – post-action identified	TBC – based on skill set needed and resource availability
06/10/2016	High	Harry	Increase traffic to 'x' section	Off-page SEO	Link to full brief	URL	URL	TBC – post-data review	TBC – post-action identified	TBC – based on skill set needed and resource availability
07/10/2016	Medium	Jane	Increase traffic to 'x' section	Link building	Link to full brief	URL	URL	TBC – post-data review	TBC – post-action identified	TBC – based on skill set needed and resource availability

Quarterly seasonal calendar

Table 8.3 details a single calendar quarter and events-based opportunities. In this case an event may be tied to industry, calendar seasons and more. When applying a quarterly calendar to your search marketing you will want to include niche events and specific seasonality tied to your industry – in this example the focus is on seasonal events (Dec/Jan/Feb).

TABLE 8.3   Quarterly seasonal calendar – events opportunity

In this case the focus is on a single quarter and types of events that may be leveraged for search engine gains – this includes example events and associated data and is by no means inclusive of every seasonal event.

Season	Winter		
Month	Dec	Jan	Feb
Key dates	Feast of the Immaculate Conception Prophet's Birthday First Day of Hanukkah Winter Solstice Christmas Day Boxing Day New Year's Eve Hogmanay	New Year's Day Burns Night Epiphany Arbor Day Plough Monday St Dwynwen's Day	Chinese New Year Shrove Tuesday Ash Wednesday Valentine's Day Random Acts of Kindness Day Ash Wednesday
Actions Examples: Blog creation Social PR Thought-leader engagement Content promotion Repurpose/re-visit previous years' content Seasonal engagement	Example actions	Example actions	Example actions
Promotions Examples: Seasonal discounts Limited time offers New product launches End-of-line promotions Limited time product ranges Guaranteed delivery dates Seasonal gifts Early entry event updates Stock clearances	Example promotions	Example promotions	Example promotions

Key Terms

Search marketing calendar

A shared resource which enables forward planning of identified important action points often spanning a number of different individual and team requirements. This helps to facilitate efficient working between disparate resources and clearly defines project needs early in the strategic planning stages of a search marketing campaign. The focus of a search marketing calendar tends to be forward-planned content needs; however, this is likely to include other expert staff in addition to a content writer, and content types will be varied. As an example of this, written content will require optimization and likely promotion – this could cover several expert staff. People creating videos, infographics or dynamic content items, are not likely to be the same specialists. All of this (and more) requires consideration and forward planning for effective implementation.

Search marketing medium

Also referred to as digital marketing mediums, or search *and* digital marketing mediums, this is the blend of marketing channels used in any single, or multiple strategies for planning to deliver online success. There are a number of search marketing channels (or mediums) and some of the most commonly used include the following:

- search engine optimization (SEO) – also known as organic advertising, natural search and free online marketing;
- pay-per-click advertising (PPC) – frequently referred to as paid adverting or sponsored search marketing;
- social media marketing – this can be paid or free and often spans specialisms. One example of this is social PR (spanning social media and traditional, digital public relations (PR));
- affiliate marketing – external business or site promotion of another company's product or service offering based on a commission earning model. Affiliates can have numerous remuneration models but often this includes driving traffic or enquiries through to another online business;
- display advertising (another branch of paid digital marketing);
- shopping channels (digital) – consider Google shopping and other specific and segmented shopping search engines solely focused on matching a search query with a product available to purchase via an ecommerce end result;

- public relations (digital) – or online PR. This can regularly be seen as an aspect of many, if not all, types of search and digital mediums used; however, it can also have a very distinct and value enhancing individual role;

- e-mail marketing – when you think about low-cost marketing, e-mail marketing is one of the first digital mediums that springs to mind. Other low-cost marketing challengers to e-mail include mobile phone marketing (SMS, or text marketing);

- mobile (tablet, Smartphone) marketing – while you could argue that most, if not all of the above can and are applicable to marketing on mobile telephones and devices, it is also possible specifically to target mobile phones as part of a wider search marketing and digital strategy, and therefore it is necessary to include them in this mediums list;

- video advertising – using video as a segmented means to market, the growth of video marketing (paid and free) as well as the user digestion of video content (not to mention the fact that the Google company also owns YouTube), demonstrates why video as a medium should not be overlooked;

- online article marketing and distribution – certainly associated to digital PR, article marketing has been a common means to leverage business, product and service updates, good news and much more, for the syndication of content effectively for many brand and business potential gains.

Digital specialisms

There are a number of distinct specialist areas when it comes to search and digital marketing (consider the list of digital marketing channels described in this sections key terms list), and most tend to result in individual experts delivering a number of specialisms, as opposed to a single person. That is not to say that one person cannot learn multiple disciplines, or deliver search marketing spanning a number of expertise areas. From experience, when working in-house, companies often look t o a single person to provide initial learning and demonstrate value, and then expand resources to deliver specialisms. Search marketing and digital agencies would often have specific teams for delivery of separate specialisms. Of course, this will differ from organization to organization

User Experience (UX)

This can be the broadest of topics or a highly niche and specific focus area of expertise. User Experience (UX) is the understanding of (in this case website) visitors' unique emotional associations to the business, product, service, medium or website. From understanding what the site is about, to knowing intuitively how to engage and interact with and use the website, UX is an area that increasing numbers of online businesses are investing in, with a view to making the most of all visitors who land on their websites. UX aims to balance and maximize the wants, needs and objectives of a user and those of a business. In an online environment, the website is frequently the main focus of end result implementation.

Content optimization

To optimize something, you enhance it and make it better. For the purposes of search engine optimization of content, you make that content accessible to search engines and users. You make the content quick to load, clearly labelled and available in various formats, to cater for universal access to it. You ensure the content has depth of information, uses the right keywords, reflects expectations and has a clear topic. Content optimization is ongoing, it never stops (although of course expert time, resource and focus will change prioritization frequently). Experts need to continue to review the data and learn from it, incrementally improving content, keeping it fresh and value added for the people digesting it. Experts make sure that the content is created based on insight and meaning, it is easy to find, promote and work towards ensuring that the content is having the desired impact (if it is not, a key part of the experts role is to change it).

Click-through rate (CTR)

The number of clicks (expressed as a percentage) compared to the number of times your organic advert has appeared (impressions).

Bounce rate

The percentage of people who leave (exit or bounce) from your website after only visiting a single page. In many cases the lower the bounce rate, the better; but there can be exceptions to this rule.

Demographics

The data that is tied towards a specific segment of the population. There are a number of metrics that can be included in demographic data including age, location, income and much more.

Key points

- Restraint is one of the biggest limitations on search success. Restraint in terms of scope, creativity, and longer term planning, all impede the potential for greater gains through search engine marketing.

- The most widely covered mutually beneficial digital relationship is between SEO and content. Every search engine optimization campaign requires the right type of content, and content cannot rely on quality alone for it to be seen by its intended audience.

- Regardless of the social media platform, the greater the success derived from social media, often the quicker and broader the search gains also received.

- One of the most confused approaches to search engine marketing is the notion that one medium completes against the other, or that, for one search channel to be a success, it has to be at the detriment to another – this simply is not true.

- When we start to consider measurements for SEO success (or metrics that matter), what is most important is identifying what matters most to you.

- A 'longer term search' calendar incorporates the core content delivery elements required to support an effective SEO campaign.

- Don't overcomplicate your longer term search calendars – you want information to be accessible for everyone involved, easy to use and understand, and effective to manage and to maximize for search marketing success.

Planning for the future

The application of specialist expertise for the purpose of increasing the quality and quantity of organic (earned, natural or free) traffic from search engines to a web page or website.

That was how we defined SEO in Chapter 1.

As we are in the final stages of the book, it is important to start looking forward to the longer term to pull together many of the topics and insights shared throughout.

LEARNING OUTCOMES

The delivery of SEO is an expert balancing act of matching tactics and opportunity with expertise and objectives, constantly reassessing the latest data, industry progression, and the niche in which you operate. With so much internal and external change and challenge constantly presenting itself, it is easy to be swept up with the *now* and never really look at the *next*.

By the end of this chapter you will have increased your awareness of:

- the constants of search marketing

- the trends for change

- the need for contingency in search engine optimization.

Understanding the constants of search marketing

In Chapter 2 we introduced the fundamentals of the Google ethos, and many of these areas could quite easily be re-positioned as the fundamentals of search engine marketing. From the Google ethos we covered:

- placing the user at the heart of strategy;
- the need for depth of specialism ('doing one thing extremely well');
- the need for speed in performance;
- universal delivery of information 'anytime, anyplace';
- making money without harming integrity;
- constant discovery of new opportunity;
- how diversity within delivery can support creativity;
- never-ending refinement and innovation.

All of the above principles are also present when we consider fundamental aspects of SEO delivery.

The topics discussed in Chapter 1, included the basic business needs that SEO fulfilled, and while the requirements for business returns from SEO tend to become ever-more inclusive, a number of these basic needs remain throughout including:

- the need to be seen in the right areas for effective search gains;
- the need to compete successfully in a challenging digital environment;
- the need to engage with your audience for mutually beneficial end results;
- the need to generate revenue and make money from your marketing investment;
- the need to fulfil a purpose – a reason for existing in this digital space.

Chapter 4 discussed the debate in relation to search mentality and weighing up longer term vs shorter term approaches. We settled on a balance that:

> Nearly all approaches to search engine optimization will be hybrids consisting of tactics available from both strategy timelines.

Some of the longer term tactics explored in Chapter 4 involved:

- website build and maintenance supporting efficient, multi-device functionality;
- data-driven content combining search engine optimization *and* user needs;
- user quality signals and social success;
- location-based expansion and maximization;
- the role of the audience, personas and context within search;
- *all* search verticals and broadening the search environment;
- linking – on-site and off-site.

If there was a single focal point for longer term success online, a constant theme that will never change, it is the need to underline the importance of *value* in almost all of the actions you complete.

Value can be used as a key counterweight to metric-only delivery – something which can often receive excessive focus and impede the wider search solution. This was summed up in Chapter 5 as:

> The excessive focus on the metric, constrains breadth of genuine value, undermines longer term success, and blinkers expertise to a point of overlooking the obvious.

A value-based approach to search engine optimization does not exclude metrics; in fact it supports their attainment. Metrics of success will be tied (certainly in part) towards bespoke goals and objectives; however, many search metrics have remained constant, and will remain so for the foreseeable future. Some of these metrics-based constants can be seen below:

- impressions;
- clicks;
- traffic (SEO, referral, direct);
- channel percentage of total website traffic;
- brand and non-brand returns;
- micro and macro goal completions.

Resource selection for SEO delivery in-house vs outsourcing, or a combination of the two, is something that has been debated for as long as SEO has existed as a specialism. This importance of this area of debate is not likely diminish and, if anything, will increase as more businesses increment the level of perceived value and general worth, that is placed on search engine optimization as a core business marketing solution.

Chapter 7 targeted this discussion point and provided a number of the more pertinent questions for businesses to self-assess, and to ask of any potential external SEO supplier. These questions and the objectives arising from them are another constant:

- What is the initial cost?
- What is the ongoing cost?
- What level of expertise will we have access to?
- How diversified is the experience of the staff?
- How integral will the people be to my business?
- How reliable is the service being delivered?
- For how long do I need to commit (to SEO)?
- How do I get the right people on board?
- How much control will I have?
- What does success look like?
- How much time goes into research and development?
- Are there any guarantees?
- What about link building (approaches/ability to service)?
- How do you decide what to focus on?
- What's the risk?
- Does exclusivity matter?
- How much time is lost in translation?
- Will expertise fade?
- How do I know if SEO is working?
- How many people will I need?
- How do we get the right content?

In Chapter 8, we focused on thinking outside of the search medium, identifying specific search metrics that matter and creating your own longer term search calendar.

At this stage, due to the focus provided on the constants of search, it may seem that very little changes with search engine optimization; however, this is far from accurate.

The next section of this chapter provides insight into recognizing the signs and trends for change in search.

Recognizing the trends for change

SEO application and the broader industry changes frequently, and a challenge for any search engine specialist is the ability constantly to learn, adapt and keep in touch with the industry as it changes.

In this section we take a deeper look at some of the recent changes in the SEO industry and provide some tips for remaining in touch (and ideally on top) of the search engine environment.

Recent SEO trends

Awareness of digital marketing change and trends can enable you repeatedly to re-assess your approach to search marketing, keep your delivery up to date, and support effectiveness by refinement of strategy and tactics deployed. While you should not just be led by industry movements, awareness is imperative to ensure that your practices are impactful (for the right reasons) and reflect the latest opportunities that present themselves to you.

Mobile

In April 2015 Google launched its mobile update, widely referred to as 'mobilegeddon' (although it has a number of other names too). This was a clear statement of intent which told businesses, website owners and search engine marketers that mobile search is *so* important that it carries ranking gains. Google has already provided a number of free mobile tools, but most applicable to this opportunity is the Mobile-Friendly Test tool, available at **www.google.com/webmasters/tools/mobile-friendly/**.

App Search (or store) Optimization (ASO)

Associated with the above, and incorporating many of the traditional elements of search engine optimization, app optimization follows the growth of the app universe and the opportunity to leverage this (as with website optimization) through free and earned forms of digital marketing. The use of mobile telephones and other handheld devices continues to grow, as will ASO.

Social SEO

Whatever term you choose to describe this trend, this basically refers to the complementary relationship and correlation of search results attributed to social engagement, sharing and content promotion. We have already seen a number of integrated search engine results pages prevailing in some of the most competitive niches online, and the consistent growth of Google-involved social media strategy (consider the purchasing of YouTube, the inclusion of Tweets in search results and more). This social SEO partnership is often omitted, but it provides great potential.

Content quality

We are truly past the daily churning of low-quality, thin content based on shallow value and even shallower purpose. From the number of words (1,000+ words seem to be an agreed minimum number for covering fairly standard topic) to interaction, easy digestion, and mixture of content types – when it comes to content creation, the trend is based on quality over quantity.

Deeper rankings

Ranking highly in the main search engines will be a long-term business search goal. This is because (ignoring personalized search and a myriad of other result-skewing factors) it is easy to understand, it is a clear 'win' over the competition, and it fuels the personal and website ego. Having said that, the use of direct answers in search results, prominence on location (consider local pack (or box) results), and other content type rankings at the top of page one results (news, images, knowledge graph/contextual results, video etc), can mean that first place does not always offer the most traffic or website value.

Artificial Intelligence (AI) and machine learning

We have seen Google launch RankBrain in quarter four of 2015 to assist with understanding and machine learning for better delivery of new (presently unclear) or currently unknown content coverage. This continued drive for AI and machine learning in Google will not slow over the next few years. Rather, it will pick up pace and we will only know about it retrospectively, as a much greater part of Google search is delivered by machines than we currently know of. This is itself a testament to its success and future potential.

Alternative communication

In this approach, we are referring to the growth of other search types over traditional text. Images are *still* one of the most neglected areas of opportunity online, and other communication search alternatives include video and voice (or spoken search). *All* of these, will build on the foundations laid, and appear more frequently and more prominently with SEO tactics and broader strategies.

Link earning

Are you receiving fewer e-mail requests for link exchanges and content swaps?

For most people, the answer to this question will be 'yes'. This is due to a shift in approach towards link creation. The goal of link building should be that you turn away from creating links, towards creating content that earns links. The best content pays for itself in many ways, one of these being natural link acquisition. Judging effective link acquisition is more a qualitative assessment of the value of the individual linking sites as opposed to the quantitative numbers game traditionally associated with link building and counting.

User focus

Whatever objective your search marketing is working towards, it will become almost impossible to ignore the end user. The days of optimizing for search (alone or in isolation from the end user) are *nearly* over, and in the next 24 months from the time of writing, it will become a greater barrier to success when you exclude the user from the approach. From personalization to persona, user-orientated tactics will become more prominent within effective SEO.

Local positioning

I predict that the power of the national (or international) brand will decline and be replaced by the power and positioning of the local brand. This does not mean that global brands will disappear; but I believe that bigger brands will need to become much more locally aware. This should be a positive trend, as national brands will need to act more like local brands and will need to compete in a local environment. This will require increasing activity with the local community, as well as providing value at local and national levels (rather than trickling down the power of national brand approaches to dominate local results with limited effort or real value).

Asking and answering

Coming back to the user, this trend is based on gathering bespoke user information and feedback, and then doing something meaningful with it. Users will give you unique insight and you will need to give them something valuable back (for free). This 'asking and answering' trend is one that is not covered much at present, but will be widely recognized in the years to come.

> How well do you know your website's users? What question would you ask them to answer? What would you do with this new information to give back something for free?

More keywords

The conversations that take place regarding the ranking for a handful of particular keywords are declining. One of the reasons for this is that people know a lot more about the value that SEO can bring outside of these 'easy-to-rank check' terms. Another reason is that many people have now achieved those handful of exact match-term rankings and questioned why they did not get much more value from them. SEO is about much more than ranking for specific keywords, and people are already realizing this – a trend that is building momentum and unlikely to ever look back. When you get past the 'rank for xyz' chat, you begin to access opportunities that are expansive and ongoing. This is revitalizing the SEO industry and will do for years to come.

Knowing whether your SEO is working

> How do you know if your search engine optimization is effective?

This is one of the widely unanswered (in fact 'unasked' is more accurate) questions that get overlooked with SEO delivery, regardless of whether the delivery is being completed in house or through outsourcing.

Part of the reason for this is that by asking this type of question the information requester is in effect asking for help. They are acknowledging that they are unsure of the answer themselves, and need to be both educated and updated on the current situation. As an aside, when you have customers (internal or external customers) who are able to ask you this type of question directly, you will likely have the type of business relationship required to support greater SEO gains.

Another aspect of this is that SEO can cover almost any trackable metric (or measurement of success). This means the idea of success can differ depending on the person looking at the metrics, and the perceived value and weight they attribute to distinct metrics.

In Chapter 8 we discussed some of the more widely used SEO metrics, and as a reminder we also cover a few of them in this section.

At this stage a good exercise would be to consider who within your business would consider each of the following as a key result measurement. Likely there will be a complete mixture of people, roles and desired metric gains – the larger the business, and the wider the set of stakeholders, the more complex the issue of understanding whether SEO is working can become.

The metrics covered next are segmented by 'quality metrics', 'quantity metrics', and 'technical plus performance metrics' – in the same way as in Chapter 8.

Quality metrics for defining SEO success include:

● Click-through rate (CTR): Are your adverts being seen by the right people? Are they relevant, targeted and incurring clicks?

● Bounce rate: What proportion of page specific and total website traffic is exiting before users view another page on your site?

● Time spent on page/site: Are visitors spending a very limited amount of time on your website? How long is a typical user journey required for a visitor to complete the desired outcome from their visit?

● Visibility and traffic relevancy: As impressions increase, are those gains resulting in extra organic (or SEO) traffic coming to your website?

● User engagement: Are users watching videos, downloading brochures, and filling out forms?

● Pages seen per visit: How much of your website content is being digested by new and return visitors?

● Demographics: Are you becoming more effective through search engine optimization in the audience areas that matter most to your business?

● End results: Micro and macro goal completions.

- Channel performance comparison: Is SEO out-performing other digital mediums?
- Price of keyword progression: Can SEO gains be seen spanning some of the more competitive search terms?

Quantity metrics for defining SEO success include:

- impressions and traffic;
- rankings and average positions;
- end results;
- percentage contributed to total site success;
- customer acquisition cost.

Chapter 8 also covered technical and wider website performance measurements of success, and these included:

- accessibility;
- access to data;
- site speed – including mobile, and devices, plus desktop;
- operability and functionality;
- website availability or uptime;
- search appearance;
- usability;
- natural linkability;
- on-page support;
- off-page support;
- search supportive;
- volume of website indexed;
- hierarchy and architecture;
- mobile site success;
- content delivery;
- internal information access.

There are many factors to consider when it comes to performance tracking, understanding and assessment. A few of those that need to be understood as part of this medium review include the following:

Progress made compared to your agreed SEO objectives

There will always be some level of disagreement when it comes to deciding what SEO is and is not accountable for improving. This is why, from the outset of any search engine optimization delivery, it is important to agree the key performance indicators, or success measurements, as early in the relationship as possible. The people you work with as part of your businesses SEO solution should be able to benchmark, measure and report on these metrics at any given stage during the process. It is also important however, to recognize that some metrics do take time to impact. Do not assume that every time an initial phase of expert actions have been completed, you will see direct, positive gains. Some objectives require a longer term focus and more actions and time to impact than others.

External factors – things that can impede, impact and remove performance

If you have worked in the SEO industry for a number of years, it will come as no surprise to hear that some projects have many more barriers to overcome before you can even get started than others. If a website has had negative algorithm impact; has suffered, or is currently suffering from a manual penalty, or (and there are many other examples of potential external factors) is many years overdue a website overhaul, this can make search engine success much more challenging. Consider a website that is not mobile friendly, the Google mobile update (also known as 'mobilegeddon'), and a website owner unwilling to invest in website updates to fulfil the basic requirements of a responsive and mobile-friendly website. If an SEO expert is working towards mobile site success with these factors in play, there will be a limit to what they can achieve.

Competitive search environment changes

Your online competition is ever changing and the commercial barriers to new entrants to the market are much lower than in many traditional business scenarios. This means that you cannot base search success just on what you are doing. In a digital environment the competitive search market can fluctuate dramatically directly impacting short, medium and longer term performance. Consider this situation.

- You sell yellow pencils.

- The mainstream media and news organizations cover a new story on the negative impact of pencils on child health. (Yes, this may be a little unlikely, but the point here is to show potential massive competitor changes online.)

- Your company was ranked number one on Google for several hundred yellow pencil related search queries.

- Overnight the top 15 search engine results are now massive media outlets (as an example BBC in the UK).

- Your SEO traffic to your website for 'pencil' themed searches drops by 85 per cent.

Is your change in SEO success in this key business area a fault of your SEO provider?

The above is a fairly extreme example of competitive search environment changes in practice; however, is it unfeasible for eBay, Amazon or other big brand ecommerce websites to start to dominate fairly niche search areas?

Business decision updates that may change performance

When you start working with any expert SEO delivery (company, individual etc) the business value, scope and potential may be different and changeable over the longer term. This can directly impact many important SEO success measurements. As an example of this, you sell screws online. You have a wide range of screws, but not all of them are profitable to your business. As a business you decide to remove any screws from your website that do not deliver a baseline return on investment (ROI). Over the three weeks this exercise takes (identifying and removing product ranges from your website), you see a 30 per cent decline in impressions, traffic and sales from your SEO. Of course you may question how the product removals were handled, and why a lot of that visibility and traffic has not been passed on to other pages on your website, but you also need to consider how your own business decisions can directly impact search performance (both positively and negatively).

The potential impact outside of SEO in isolation

You should not just look at the SEO segment of data to come to a decision on the progress of SEO as a digital medium. When you increase the value of site content and make it more linkable, you support referral traffic gains. When you effectively improve brand reach and awareness, you almost always bring more direct website traffic to a business. These are just two possible examples where SEO success (in a situation that does not account for the broader positive impact of SEO) can be overlooked.

Repositioning your visibility

If you are massively visible in areas your business does not want to cater for, and you task SEO experts to help you reposition your website online, it is possible that this may negatively impact almost every search engine success measurement over the short to medium term. This goes back to measuring SEO, based on your unique objectives. More impressions and traffic are a frequently used gauge of SEO success. However, if you are being seen for the wrong search terms, and you are appearing before the wrong target audiences, you need to change. Repositioning can mean lower visibility, fewer visits, but potentially more business value and end results, including increased ROI. As an example of this. If your business sells luxury household goods with an average order value of £3,000, the potential audience is massively reduced compared to a business selling household goods with an average order value of £50 pounds. The fact is, however, that both businesses will have an audience that enables SEO to deliver business ROI, but the measurements of success, tied to effective positioning, will be very different.

Putting your contingency plan in place

There is no reason to set aside a contingency plan based on any assumption of total SEO failure.

There is always a successful route to market with search engine optimization – your contingency plans can therefore help you to identify these alternatives and to utilize them effectively.

Your search contingency plan helps mitigate risk of failure from any primary SEO outcome, and encourages risk reduction within your strategy.

The main questions that should be answered in a search contingency plan are listed below.

The purpose of asking these questions from the outset, is to answer them early on, and reflect the solutions within your strategy for a more robust approach to delivering results with search engine optimization:

- What is the biggest threat to my SEO strategy?
- How can we plan for (or avoid) this main threat (or sets of identified threats) occurring?
- What have we missed?
- What if things change? How can we prepare for the unknown?
- What preparation can be done to react to any SEO failure and implement contingency?
- What will be the minimum expected return? (Note – 'return' is not just capital return but, value, content, website, business, user etc.)
- What is the worst case scenario? How can we plan to avoid this?
- How are we restricting our ability to succeed in search?

There are a number of ways to create a contingency plan, but as they are so directly linked to your objectives, it seems more useful to provide you with tips for creating your search (or rather SEO) contingency plan instead of just providing one example to replicate.

Here are some tips to get you going with your own SEO contingency plan – the litmus test is to ask yourself if they answer the questions set out above, or not.

Measurements

Your contingency plans should have metrics attributed to them. Everyone involved in the project should know what success and failure looks like, so that strategy can incorporate this logic into the approach. Success (and failure) needs to be quantified and ideally discussed and agreed on. Maintaining search success could be an objective for one company, as well as a total disaster for another.

Event triggers

To change approach or implement items from a contingency plan (unless doing so proactively as opposed to reactively), you need to have some form of process and a means to trigger events from the plan. For example, traffic reduces by 20 per cent, conversions decline by 25 per cent etc.

Prioritized actions

When you have a number of supplemental and currently unused performance contingencies, you need to be able logically to assess them and prioritize them. Some actions may require additional spend, while others take longer to facilitate implementation. All of these aspects, and many more need to be considered, so that when you decide to act upon, or include elements of contingency in your strategy, you can do so effectively.

Revisit and refresh

Your contingency plan, like any other strategy item, could become dated and fail to reflect current needs. Setting regular review, refresh and revisit sessions is important to the potential impact of any plan you have drawn up.

Culture inclusion

Contingency, crisis management, back-up plans (or any other term you see in relation to this topic) need to be reflected in the attitude and the culture of the business in which you operate. Contingency requires buy-in and support from key decision makers and influencers, including the people most likely to be called upon to implement contingency plans.

Ownership and accountability

Every action in your approach to contingency requires ownership of task, overseeing and implementation. For contingency, staff required should also have added resource in case of staff change plus any external requirements for short-term support.

Key points

- As we are in the final stages of this book it is important to start looking forward to the longer term to pull together many of the topics and insights shared throughout.
- With so much internal and external change and challenge constantly presenting itself, it is easy to be swept up with the *now* and never really look at *the next*.
- If there was a single focal point for longer term success online, a constant theme is the need to place importance of *value* in almost all of the actions you complete.

- SEO application and the broader industry change frequently, and a challenge for any search engine specialist is the ability constantly to learn, adapt and keep in touch with the industry as it changes.

- While you should not just be led by industry movements, awareness is imperative to ensure that the practices you use are impactful and reflect the latest opportunities that present themselves to you.

- There is always a successful route to market with search engine optimization – your contingency plans can therefore help you to identify these alternatives and to utilize them effectively.

INDEX

Page numbers in *italic* indicate figures.